Gianni Versace

Fashion's Last Emperor

First published in Great Britain in 1997 by Essential

24 Conway Street

London W1P 5HP

in association with Chameleon Books

an imprint of Andre Deutsch Ltd

106 Great Russell Street

London WC1B 3LJ

Andre Deutsch Ltd is a subsidiary VCI plc

Printed and bound in Italy.

A catalogue record for this book is available from the British Library.

ISBN 0233 993 428

Gianni Versace

Fashion's Last Emperor

Lowri Turner

Gianni Versace

introduction

I first met Gianni Versace in 1992. His face was already familiar from the glossy advertising brochures and public relations material that regularly crossed my desk at the *Evening Standard* newspaper in London. Minimalist black-and-white snaps of the stubbly-cheeked designer were slipped between umbrellas and Wales, Prince of (the checked fabric, not the person) in my office filing system.

In Paris and Milan, I would study Versace again – from a distance of a few feet and in full colour. He would take to the runway at the end of his shows with a slightly harassed air and a Supermodel hanging off each arm. I would be sitting in the audience, a monumentally uncomfortable gilt chair having worn a groove in the one buttock it was big enough to support, watching and scribbling in my notebook. I'd be trying simultaneously to lip-read what Christy, Cindy or Marpessa had just said to the maestro and attempting to get a closer look at the beading on the skirt of a dress that was flitting past me much too quickly – was that a 'Marilyn Monroe' worked in iridescent glass beads?

Back in any of a series of Parisian or Milanese hotel rooms, I

would examine Gianni once more. Pictures of his collection were hurriedly developed in the bathroom by my catwalk cohort, photographer Ken Towner, using small bottles of noxious-smelling liquid and a complicated arrangement of light-proof containers and the sort of black bags from which magicians pull rabbits. The results would be laid out on a portable light-box. This time it would be me who was harassed as I tried to select images to wire back to London. The wire machine would be making ominous beeping noises, the phone line would go down and I would be staring through a magnifier or 'Lupe' at Versace's features reversed and tinged in a luminous shade of green by the colour negative film.

Until 1992, however, I had never actually met the man himself. And I didn't expect to. Gianni Versace's clothes were the first I ever saw on a big designer catwalk. The first time I spied Naomi Campbell close enough to wonder at the length of her thighs or Linda Evangelista and marvelled at the improbability of her latest hair colour, they were wearing Versace. I was the newly-appointed Fashion Editor of London's *Evening Standard* newspaper and when I was not being fascinated by this strange breed of human coat-hanger, just starting to be called 'The Supermodel', I was stunned by the clothes.

Versace's autumn/winter 1990 collection seemed to be all flash and flesh with acres of rhine-stones, yards of leather and models walking down the runway while taking all this stuff off in a manner that I had presumed was reserved for lapdancers earning $20 a shimmy. Being a Milan fashion virgin, I reported it all, employing the word 'stripper'. This didn't go down at all well with the Versace organization. Next season I was shifted back a row in the all-important feature pecking order.

However, as I clocked up bannings from fashion houses in Milan, Paris, London and New York over the years (their revenge for my unkind comments), glossy, baroque print invitations from Versace continued to arrive. Other designers might have been gripped by the sort of insecurity that leads them to try to muzzle the press, but Versace was clever and classy enough not to try. And I respected him for that.

OK, so the crisp carrier bags containing this season's $5,000 complimentary suit that I saw being delivered to other fashion editors didn't come my way. I was never invited over to one of his stores and requested to select something from the racks. But I was, on one occasion, the recipient of a hilariously over-the-top Versace ashtray. I rather fancied stubbing out Silk Cuts on the lavish design. Unfortunately, it was stolen from my hotel room before I could get it home. Even maids in Milan can spot a good designer freebie when they see it.

It was with this chequered history in mind that I approached Versace's 'people' in 1992 and asked for an interview. Chief among the terrifying wall of women who surrounded the Emperor was Emmanuella Schmeidler, Head of International Public Relations. Slim as a whippet but with sharper claws, stories of Emmanuella ripping up show tickets in front of weeping fashion editors abounded. The facts that the opening of Versace's new London flagship store was imminent and that I was Fashion Editor of London's Donatella and a whole gaggle of other terrifying women in very small skirts and with very big hair. This was the Versace court. Precious minutes passed as I was plied with chi-chi patisserie (which I don't eat) and English tea (which I don't drink) by Gianni's acolytes. After the small talk — how gorgeous Claudia was looking after her holiday in Monaco, how fabulous Sting's new single was — the meaning of this little *tête-à-tête* became clear.

'What is vulgar? I don't know what vulgar is!'

only newspaper would, I considered, improve my chances of a one-to-one chat from that of a cat in hell, but only slightly. When the answer came back and it was 'Yes', I was flabbergasted.

I arrived at the appointed meeting place — the lobby of a swish hotel in Milan — on time. Gianni was nowhere to be seen. Instead I was faced with the massed ranks of Emmanuella, Gianni's equally intimidating sister

I was being softened up before my audience with the maestro, although that is perhaps too pastel a term for what was really going on. Like a pride of lionesses protecting an especially sickly cub, they were sizing me up to see what damage I might do to their precious charge. 'Gianni is very tired,' I was told, 'He has been working too hard,' I was informed, before they hit me with the question that clinched my suspicions, 'What exactly are you going to ask him?', they enquired with a mixture of sweetness and intimidation. I blustered and skirted around the subject, all the while conscious of the butter knife that was neatly placed within the perilously easy reach of Ms Schmeidler.

I must have passed muster, or perhaps they just gave up, because I was finally taken up to Gianni's suite. It was grand, but nowhere near as luxurious as the pictures of the Emperor's many palaces which regularly appeared in magazines. There were no Picassos or Fernand Lègers on the walls and no leopard print cushions or Corinthian columns — just a lot of hotel-issue, reproduction nineteenth-century furniture in mahogany veneer. Gianni was evidently slumming it. Not that he appeared a bit miffed by his surroundings. He greeted me courteously, if a little shyly and we sat down by a window, next to a low coffee table decorated with brochures advertising the delights of Milan. One of his PR people continued to hover in the background, 'just in case he needed a little help with his English', I was informed.

When interviewing celebrities it is customary for the retinue that surrounds them to be fearsome and for the stars themselves to be as nice as pie. This has very little to do with the genuine state of affairs. Rather, it is an arrangement that is constructed entirely for the interviewee's benefit; to make him or her appear delightful, while getting others to do the dirty work of being difficult and demanding on their behalf. 'Oh, but Mr or Ms X is so nice when you actually get to meet them. It's just their agent/PR who's a nightmare' is a common interviewer's refrain.

But you don't build a billion-dollar company by being Mary Poppins. And besides, fiery fallings-out between Gianni, Santo and Donatella were hardly a secret. Yet the Gianni Versace that I met was nice — very nice, in fact. Wearing a black polo neck and trousers, he looked like a cheerful, hamster-cheeked beatnik. He was softly spoken and charmingly self-deprecating. Only once did he appear short-tempered. When I asked him if he felt that the characterization of some of his designs as vulgar was fair, he threw his hands up in the air and demanded, 'What is vulgar? I don't know what vulgar is!'.

Gianni Versace

Do not disturb

*The Emperor in black leather with Naomi and Claudia
(sporting frizzed hair).*

However, Versace didn't really want to talk about fashion. He preferred to discuss art or music. 'My dream was always to be a composer, but fashion came very easily,' he told me. 'Music is still very important to me.' He was due to go off on tour with Elton John to act not only as Wardrobe Mistress to Elton's exuberant stage wardrobe, but also as Art Director for the entire production. The prospect evidently excited him. When I expressed doubts as to how he might continue to run his business if he was schlepping around the world with his rock star mate he sighed, 'I want to take time off,' he said. 'I don't want to make money, more money. I want to better myself.'

Here was a man, I felt, who was to some degree a prisoner of his own success. He was on a treadmill, producing two couture collections a year, four ready-to-wear (two men's, two women's) and countless diffusion, sports and accessories collections, not to mention the houseware line and the perfumes. Clearly, he'd had enough and he wanted to do other things. By the end of our interview I had decided that either Gianni was very tired indeed, or he was having some sort of mid-life crisis. When he said, 'I want to be like Greta Garbo and say "Basta!" ', the possibility that he might rename himself Stardust Moonchild and decamp to Goa to run a Kaftan stall seemed entirely plausible. But of course he didn't. Versace's world, the one he had built, was one of palaces, not hammocks on a beach. And if he had taken up residence in the latter, then somehow you just knew that he would have had to redesign it with a gold filigree border.

When, back in my somewhat less palatial hotel room, I sat down to write up the interview, I thought about everything he'd said. Did I like the Gianni Versace I met? Yes, a lot. Did I vow never to criticize his clothes ever again and instead to bow down before his designs in Islamic adoration thenceforth? Not exactly, but I certainly understood his approach to design better. Did I think that if he ever did bow out of the fashion world that it would be a loss?

Absolutely. GV

A Calabrian Dawn

There isn't much glitz in Reggio de Calabria. Anyone unwise enough to try taking a turn along the waterfront promenade in a pair of psychedelic Greco—Roman print leggings and a beaded bra top would cause, if not quite a stir (the local populace's preferred expression is a hard, unwavering stare), then suspicions would certainly be aroused. They don't like outsiders in Reggio de Calabria. And they like flashy outsiders even less.

And yet it was here, fifty years ago, that Gianni Versace was born. Here, among the squat, functional buildings, arranged along monotonously straight streets, that fashion's most extravagantly exotic designer drew his first tentative sketches. As the young Gianni surveyed his depressing surroundings, made even more gloomy by the preponderance of beige concrete (we're talking an Eastern Bloc housing project without the charm), did he dream of Linda Evangelista in a lilac-spangled mini skirt or Cindy Crawford in a plunge-front vermilion satin evening gown? As he perhaps gazed up at the city's cathedral — solid and charmless — did he fantasize about having his own private palaces, stuffed with antiques, old masters and enough leopard print to clothe a medium-sized African country, and lavish enough to entertain princesses

An early portrait of the young Gianni Versace.

dressed in silver sequins and queens in pink leather?

It is significant that the one stunningly beautiful view available to the inhabitants of Reggio de Calabria is away from the city, across the clear blue waters of the straits of Messina to Sicily. If Gianni did look out to sea and vow to seek his fortune elsewhere, then he was not the first. Calabria has a long history of emigration. There are more Calabrese in the USA than in Italy.

To some extent, this is due to cruelty on the part of Mother Nature. If southern California seems an unfortunate place in which to build a beach house, Reggio de Calabria is even more dodgy a location in which to set up home. Situated on the western tip of the toe (and a heavily calloused one at that) of the Italian boot, it is regularly riven by natural disasters. The Aspromonte mountains that it straddles are battered by vicious storms and mud slides. Reggio itself is prone to earthquakes. The last really big one in 1908 flattened the whole city, hence the ugly concrete utilitarianism of the current architecture.

When it has not been under natural attack, Reggio de Calabria has provided fertile soil for invading armies. It was the Greeks

Versace A-Z

Shortly before Versace's death, it was reported that he had agreed to appear in a forthcoming movie, written and directed by Woody Allen. The man who had dressed so many actors, including Rupert Everett, Dolph Lundgren, Sly Stallone and Hugh Grant, and kitted out the entire cast of glossy 1980's TV series *Miami Vice*, was to have stepped in front of the camera to play himself. Filming was due to start in the autumn of 1997.

A is for Allen

who established a walled city on the site in 750 BC, naming it Rhegium. They were followed by the Normans, Arabs and Spaniards. By the nineteenth century, bitter internal wars and repeated outbreaks of malaria had resulted in general anarchy, with bandits holed up in the mountains and preying on whatever peasants remained below. Today, the Calabrese Mafia, '*ndragheta*' in local dialect, exercise a hold over the people that is even stronger than the infamous Sicilian Mafia or Neapolitan Camorra hold over their relatively more prosperous local constituencies.

The effect of Reggio de Calabria's turbulent history on the population (currently standing at 160,000) has been profound. There is a frontier air about the place, with its inhabitants displaying a doggedness and, to the outsider at least, a singular lack of a sense of humour. Would Gianni Versace have become the focused man he was, had he not come from this rough location? Certainly, the area's bitter legacy appears to have left its mark, and not just on Gianni, but on his sister Donatella and brother Santo as well.

Early pictures of Gianni show a serious-faced little boy in a white first communion suit. His expression, uncomfortable but determined, is one that is often seen on the streets of Reggio de Calabria and one that he would later display on the catwalk as he walked out in front of the audience to receive his applause. With his unshaven cheeks decorated with scarlet lipstick kisses from his Supermodel retinue and with more kisses being blown by the celebrities lining the front row of his show, Gianni remained tense. A smile (if there was one) was thin. Here was a man who was not about to be swept up in the adoration. He had tomorrow's *Women's Wear Daily* report to worry about.

Santo Versace invariably wears an even sterner version of this quintessentially Calabrian stare, and as for Donatella, her smooth, tanned features may crease into a toothsome grin as she greets Sting and Trudie, Sly and Jennifer, but the look in her eyes is steely. That is not to say that the Versaces were (or are) cold in private. Vicki Woods, former Editor of British *Harpers & Queen* magazine, now Contributing Editor of American *Vogue* says, 'They are a great, big, noisy, spaghetti-cooking, ice-cream-

eating Italian family.' The three siblings enjoyed a fiery relationship, but they were devoted to one another, all the more so perhaps as a result of a childhood tragedy.

Gianni Versace was born on 2 December 1946. He was the second child of Antonio and Francesca Versace. Francesca had given birth to Santo three years earlier. Calabrian families are traditionally large and, indeed, a much-wanted daughter duly

All dressed up and somewhere to go. Gianni in his first communion suit.

followed the two boys. Would she, too have joined her older brothers in the fashion business? It was not to be. A mystery surrounds exactly what happened, but what is known is that she died while still a child. Donatella's birth, eight years after Gianni's, was, according to sources close to the family, an effort by her grief-stricken parents to replace their first beloved daughter.

Even allowing for a southern Italian distrust of outsiders, the degree of closeness displayed by the surviving adult Versace offspring was striking. Catwalk photographer Christopher Moore has watched their rise since the beginning. He describes them as being 'like a circus family'. They may have bickered amongst themselves and the rows between Gianni and Santo were legendary, but when attacked by others they were fiercely protective of each other, the loss of one sister having perhaps made them even more mindful of the preciousness of the sibling bond.

Gianni, Santo and Donatella were raised, if not in poverty, then in simple surroundings, a world away from the ostentatious luxury of their later lifestyles. Post-war Reggio de Calabria was once

again in a state of flux, having been heavily bombed by the allies during World War Two, and Antonio Versace's income from selling appliances was hardly in the private plane league. Francesca supplemented the family income by running her own dress salon.

It was in Francesca's small boutique that Gianni's interest in fashion was first sparked.

Watching the small contingent of Reggio de Calabria's well-heeled signoras click in and out of the shop, trying on locally-made copies of Dior's New Look, he had an ideal opportunity to eavesdrop on the world of women and clothes. Gianni never went to fashion school. He got his education by standing amongst the racks of clothes in his mother's shop and listening to the customers talk about their lives and how fashion fitted into them.

What he learnt there he never forgot. If he later became famous for fantastical evening gowns with fabulously plunging necklines, their construction — ingenious use of straps and pre-formed cups stitched into the inside — was testament to his understanding of the figure problems of real women, albeit

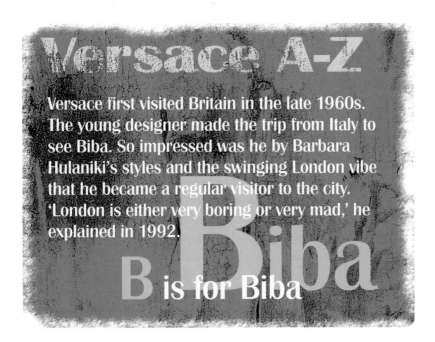

Versace first visited Britain in the late 1960s. The young designer made the trip from Italy to see Biba. So impressed was he by Barbara Hulaniki's styles and the swinging London vibe that he became a regular visitor to the city. 'London is either very boring or very mad,' he explained in 1992.

B is for Biba

ones below an American standard size sixteen.

At first, Francesca's younger son was left to play quietly in a corner with offcuts of fabric while his mother got on with the serious business of selling frocks. Later, he was dispatched to choose embroideries in Messina. 'I took the ferry and each time I tried to choose more beautiful and extraordinary materials,' he wrote in his book *Signatures*. Any money left over was spent on an ice-cream eaten on the ferry on the way back. Bearing in mind Versace's famous taste for the richly Baroque, it is tempting to imagine the scene when the young Gianni returned from his trip, his stomach full of *gelato* and his arms laden with fabulous fabrics. Was he scolded for being too over-the-top for Reggio de

Calabria's provincial clientèle? Presumably, he got the balance between fantasy and reality right, for his mother continued to send him on her fashion errands.

Versace's creativity blossomed at an early age. He began by fashioning the tiny scraps of material that he found on the workroom floor into puppets to amuse the clientèle. At the precociously young age of nine, however, he branched out. In a style emulating the kind of Hollywood glamour that would become his trademark, Gianni designed his first dress which was a one-shouldered evening gown made from velvet. His interest in fashion extended to Donatella's appearance. At the age of ten, he announced that his baby sister should have her hair highlighted. Donatella, obviously much in thrall to her sophisticated elder brother, promptly went to the hairdresser and demanded streaks. Her hair remains defiantly blonde to this day.

When not in the shop or at home, the Versace family took trips up into the mountains. It was on one of these outings, in 1959, that Gianni posed for another picture. Again stern-faced, he stands, the profile that Hilary Alexander, Fashion Editor of London *Daily* and *Sunday Telegraph* newspapers says, 'could have been stamped on an imperial Roman coin', turned firmly to the camera. His hands are placed in his pockets in a typical teenage *ennui* pose, although whether the woolly hat that he wears is an early fashion statement or simply a cold weather precaution is left open to question.

Fodder for Gianni's growing fascination with fashion was not confined to his family and the family business. Reggio de Calabria was also home to another type of woman – one who did not wear little tweed suits with a matching hat and handbag. Gianni famously

revealed that one of his greatest early influences was the local brothel. He described the prostitutes as 'beautiful, magical women'. In later years, he had reason to regret this confession. It fed the image of Versace as the designer of flashy hooker-wear for wealthy women who wanted to look cheap. Still, to a young man, surrounded by the greyness of post-war, bombed-out Reggio de Calabria, the bright colours and raunchy silhouettes modelled by the local ladies of the night must have appeared incredibly exotic. Maybe not quite glamorous, even tatty close up, but they were vibrantly exciting all the same.

The other great inspiration for the couturier in embryo was Calabria's Greek heritage. 'I come from a land with a rich history, from Magna Grecia, full of vivacity. It's roots are old, ancient roots, that knew the aristocracy of sculptural draperies', Gianni wrote many years later in *Signatures*, the first of a glossy series of books produced by the Versace Group. Gianni was indeed brought up in a house next to the ruins of a Greek

One of his greatest early influences was the local brothel.

He described the prostitutes as 'beautiful, magical women'.

Teenage Gianni models sweater and woolly hat (1959).

'They are a great, big, noisy, spaghetti-cooking, ice-cream-eating Italian family.'

Vicki Woods, Contributing Editor, American *Vogue*

temple. However, if this conjures up images of the young, short-wearing Gianni picking his way among fragments of intricate mosaic, the truth is rather less romantic. Few physical signs of Rhegium remain in Reggio de Calabria, having been destroyed by war and earthquakes. Small sections of the original city wall and a hint of the Roman baths are all that are left.

For concrete proof of the city's classical heritage, rather than just concrete, Gianni would have had to travel north along the Corso Garibaldi to the Museo Nazionale della Magna Grecia. The exterior is impressive, if not exactly festooned with Versace's favourite *Up Pompei*-style design features. It was erected in Mussolini's time and the building is Fascist architecture at its most imposing. Inside, however, it houses the finest collection of Greek antiquities south of Naples. Statues, jewellery, vases, glass, coins, scraps of architectural decoration and mosaics – it doesn't take the mind of Sherlock Holmes to work out where Gianni got the idea for his trademark Greco–Roman detailing from.

Two exhibits seem to have proved a particularly rewarding study for the keen young designer. One, a terracotta Acroterion (a nude boy astride a horse with his feet supported by a Sphinx) is but a gilded Medusa head button's toss away, stylistically-speaking, from the sort of heroic Versace advertising campaigns created by photographers Richard Avedon and Bruce Weber.

Then there are the Ex-Voto plaques. Taken from the sanctuary of Persephone at Mannella, Locri, they depict the Greek goddess Persephone bathing, having her hair done and getting dressed. How Gianni must have pored over the exquisite draping of Persephone's Greek robes, the fineness of her jewellery and the intricacy of her embroidery. Eerily similar details have resurfaced many times on the Versace catwalk — leather jackets trimmed with geometric embroidery, metal mesh mini dresses draped into quasi togas, rhinestone-studded, stiletto-heeled Roman sandals — all worn by Versace's very own fashion goddesses, Naomi, Cindy, Christy, Linda *et al*.

Gianni continued to polish his skills. He worked for his mother until the age of twenty-five and learnt tailoring in her workroom and selling in the shop. But it wasn't enough. High fashion was still regarded as an almost exclusively French preserve, the label made in Paris remaining the supreme mark of cachet.

A Versace family gathering. Gianni is, as ever, at the centre of things.

However, the stranglehold of France on style was weakening. London was swinging and labels such as Biba and Mary Quant proved that there was life beyond the Rue Faubourg St Honoré. The Italian garment industry was also emerging as a genuine force. If Mussolini made the trains run on time, then his legacy was an Italian manufacturing industry who were proving that they could also deliver on time.

Gianni wanted to be part of the new Italian fashion wave, but that couldn't happen if he stayed in Reggio de Calabria. He had to

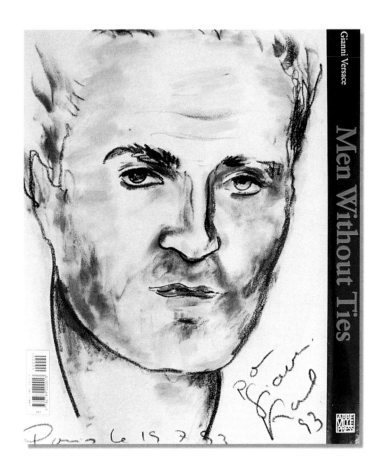

The back cover of Versace's Men Without Ties *(Abbeville Press).*

Versace A-Z

Some questioned Versace's decision to establish a home on Miami's outré South Beach. He brushed aside concerns for his safety. 'Here, in Miami I don't want another monastery to live in, I want a place to read Truman Capote,' he said.

Capote
C is for Capote

go north. His chance came in 1972. Salvatore Chiodini was an agent and Ezio Nicosia the owner of the Florentine Flowers factory in Lucca. The pair were ahead of their time in realizing that the era of bland clothing was over. Now the customer was looking for fashion with a recognizable signature, but who was to supply this added ingredient? It was Chiodini who persuaded Nicosia to try out a young, unknown tailor from the deep south. On 5 February 1972, Gianni Versace boarded a plane at Reggio de Calabria's and set off for Milan.

Gianni's first job was to bolster the existing summer range. Florentine salesman, travelling round the country with suitcases stuffed full of samples, added in a few of Versace's ideas and immediately reported enthusiastic reactions from buyers. Nicosia augmented Gianni's agreed four million lire salary with a shiny new VW convertible. But this was not enough to hold the ambitious designer. After completing his first full collection for Florentine Flowers — an autumn/winter line which was again very well-received — he made his escape.

The next two years saw Gianni Versace making a series of moves.

After Florentine Flowers, he transferred to Parisini of Santa Margherita. He made a brief visit home. However, after the glamour and sophistication of the north he had no intention of settling down again in a southern backwater. He boarded another plane and began work at Callaghan in Novara. This is the company that later discovered Romeo Gigli. It was a high-profile appointment. Still, Gianni was restless. The next rung on the career ladder was Alma in Bareggio, just outside Milan, then he moved again, this time to Genny and Complice.

In a neat irony, Complice is today famous for being the line designed by Dolce & Gabbana, the Italian duo who most often share Madonna's wardrobe credits with Gianni Versace. Their style is effervescent in the extreme — mock pony skin trouser suits, accessorized with several metres of pearl rope and topped off with a truck-load of diamanté crucifixes. However, Dolce & Gabbana have merely inherited Versace's fashion mantle. Complice was a label created specifically for Gianni. As such, it was a major step forward for him. For the first time in his career, he had creative control. **GV**

On To Milan

In 1978, the fashion industry was smaller, less sophisticated and not as global as it is today. The Eastern Bloc still languished behind the 'Iron Curtain'. China was a closed world. Designers had yet to become brands, franchizing themselves internationally like fast food chains. If the opportunities for a young, ambitious designer were narrower, there were fewer 'frockmeisters' about. The rag trade had yet to fully acquire its hyper-glamour image. Fashion schools were not pumping out the volume of aspiring couturiers that they do today.

Competition was simply not as fierce at the time. That said, for Gianni Versace to leave the safe embrace of his job at Complice was quite a risk. Could he make an impact? And would he be able to make a living?

Versace's first step was to find someone he could trust to handle the business side of the operation. As would become the pattern in the life of the fashion emperor, he turned to his family.

While Gianni had been building up a reputation for design, his elder brother Santo's talents had been

focused in a different direction. A graduate of Messina University in business administration, in 1972 Santo had opened up his own management consultancy in Reggio de Calabria. Any thoughts of staying at home and striking out on his own disappeared, however, with the news that Gianni was planning to launch his own label.

The brothers' skills complemented each other perfectly. Gianni, the flamboyant couturier with his head full of grand visions, was tempered by Santo's sound business sense. As Vicki Woods, former Editor of British *Harpers & Queen* and now Contributing Editor of American *Vogue*, says, 'Santo is the one who worries about the business.' In later years, as Gianni made last minute adjustments to outfits backstage at one of his fashion shows, tugging down a hemline here, rearranging a necklace there, Santo would be front of house, shrewdly observing the crowds arriving. As the buyers from Bergdorf Goodman and Barneys in New York, Harvey Nichols and Harrods in London, plus representatives of every other prestigious store in the world filed in, Santo would stand silently. Was he calculating the gross worth of their combined budgets and what percentage of that figure might be secured?

A portrait of Santo Versace, the ever-serious older brother.

Gianni Versace

(Above)
Sweater dress glamour
Autumn/Winter 1980
(Above right)
Leather equestrian chic
Autumn/Winter 1980.

Like Gianni before him, in 1976 Santo had packed his bags and boarded a plane for Milan. At first, he worked only part-time for Gianni as the two plotted their strategy. The most pressing problem was to find a showroom and store for the new label. In 1978, they found it on Via della Spiga. Milan's most glamorous shopping street, Via della Spiga, is smaller and more meandering than New York's Fifth Avenue, and similar in character to London's Bond Street. Today, it is lined by boutiques bearing some of the biggest names in international fashion, between which flit Milan's wealthy men and women, clanking with expensive jewellery and sporting all-weather sunglasses, and

' "Drop dead glamour" was an expression synonymous with Gianni Versace's clothes. "To-die-for frocks" was another,' Judy Rumbold wrote in the British *Guardian* newspaper. 'That throwaway remarks as pithy as these might ever be credited with even a shred of literal meaning will be a sobering thought for the fashion industry mourning the loss of one of its favourite characters.'

D is for Drop Dead Glamour

accumulating shiny carrier bags. The air is filled with competing designer perfumes and aftershaves, but even these cannot stifle the overwhelming smell of money.

Today those men and women are likely to be spending heavily in Versace. His is the name that is synonymous with the slick and expensive look of modern Milanese style. But back in the spring of 1978, when Gianni and Santo picked up the keys to their new premises, they had nothing to sell. Having secured an exclusive address, they had no line with which to fill this elegant new store. So, for the first season, the garments hanging on the racks inside bore the labels Genny, Callaghan and Complice, rather than that of Gianni Versace.

The first Gianni Versace collection for men and women was launched at the Palazzo della Permanente in Milan at the end of 1978. The magic Gianni had worked on the Florentine Flowers collection six years before was worked once more.

Strip away the gloss and glamour and fashion is like any other manufacturing industry. For a new product, be it a breakfast cereal or a designer label to be successful it must provide

Jerry Hall was one of Versace's earliest catwalk queens;
(Above) **In un-buttoned shirt with headscarf** *Spring/Summer 1982*
(Left) **Gianni gets creative with a scarf** *Spring/Summer 1982.*

'Style makes sense only if it is your own,'

Gianni Versace in

Men Without Ties

something that is not already there – either that or do it more cheaply. Gianni was not interested in undercutting his rivals. From the start, his clothes were breathlessly luxurious. While it is true that later he may have launched a profusion of cheaper diffusion lines and mass produced tee-shirts, their creation was dependent on the clear and highly recognizable design signature so richly established in his original ranges. He sold sex and glamour and he sold it with the gusto of the most garrulous second-hand car dealer.

Certainly, Gianni's early ranges were neither so lavish nor so obviously rock 'n' roll as they became in later years. The psychedelic Baroque prints were absent; the gold quota was well down. A slightly Japanese flavour was even evident in the use of origami-esque folded sleeves and architectural pleated hoods. Still, there was nothing really weird about his clothes. Not for him Rei Kawakubo three sleeves or no-sleeves-at-all styling. Fraying seams, tattered hems and blotchy dyeing were not Versace's thing.

There was always a polish, a sophistication and a thread of modernity in his early lines, the same one that continues to weave its way through Versace's many ranges of designs today. This meant a sharp silhouette rather

Bare faced (and bottomed) cheek from Versace's Men Without Ties (Abbeville Press).

than an unwearable costume.

Photographer Christopher Moore has been setting up his camera next to catwalks in Milan, Paris, New York and London for thirty years. He says of Versace's first collections, 'I don't know if his things were ever exactly quiet, but he was more subdued.' In part, this may have had something to do with the times. The disco era was ending and fashion was in a sort of limbo. The flamboyance of the New Romantics, the nightclub cult which sparked a wave of mass

market frills and flounces, and influenced the design of Lady Diana's wedding dress by David and Elizabeth Emmanuel, had not yet arrived. The power-dressed Dynasty diva, whose slick and sexy style was made for Versace, was not even on the horizon.

Still, if Versace was constrained by his times and the fact that he was a new designer with limited resources, his vision was clear. 'Style makes sense only if it is your own,' he later wrote in *Men Without Ties*. Slinky dresses in black and silver and flashes of

Porsche red poured off his catwalk. The Grecian influence emerged quickly. Toga-style dresses featured almost from the start. However, Versace's true skill was in interpreting rather than in copying classical images. 'I'm not nostalgic and instead I have a sense of the future that pervades my fashion,' he wrote in *Signatures*.

This attempt to create something new, while referring to the past, is the mark of every great designer. Vivienne Westwood, for example, has plundered everything from Tudor doublet and hose to Scottish clansman's attire, yet manages to create garments with an essential modernity. Versace's fashion heroines were Balenciaga and Chanel, both of whose careers were marked by a need for newness. Gianni, too, constantly sought to move fashion forward. 'What will 2001, the future which is practically present, be like? How will these exciting and difficult years affect us when everything changes so turbulently,' he mused in the brochure accompanying a *Versus* collection.

To look at the history of fashion in terms of hemlines and silhouettes is only to tell half the story. What really drives style is not a drawing on a page, but a vat in a factory. Fabric technology is at the root of every new look. Versace knew this. 'I used to try to select fabrics and prints for my mother's clients and they never seemed new enough for me, and I felt there should be something more,' he reminisced in *Signatures*. So, just as he had journeyed from Reggio de Calabria to Messina for his mother, collecting fabrics for her shop, once he had established his own fashion house he sought new materials with which to work.

In 1982, he made his first really big breakthrough. Gianni created a totally new fabric, his now-famous chain mail. The Lycra of its time, Versace's remarkable invention slithered over the body like liquid gold. It was fine enough to gather without being bulky, yet had a weight that made it mould to a woman's curves. Quite simply, it is one of the sexiest fabrics ever to hit a catwalk. Versace's chain mail put him firmly on the fashion map. In 1982, he won the first of a series of *L'Occhio d'Oro* awards (Italian fashion Oscars) for Best Womenswear Designer. He began experimenting in earnest with fur and silk, leather and lace. The full-on Versace style was beginning to

Versace A-Z

Despite Linda Evangelista being one of Versace's favourite models, her taste for practical jokes could backfire on the family. On one occasion, Evangelista sneaked Gianni's niece Allegra, then nine, onto the catwalk. Afterwards, as Donatella tore a terrifying strip off her daughter, according to onlookers Evangelista 'was laughing fit to bust'.

E is for Evangelista

emerge. Still, there was one piece of the jigsaw that had yet to fall into place. And that piece came with a capital 'D' on it, inscribed in solid gold leaf.

'He already had a point of view, but before Donatella arrived in the late Eighties he didn't have the pizzazz or the panache. He just took off,' says Christopher Moore. Donatella's arrival was important in two ways. First, on a personal level, she completed the Versace triumvirate. The siblings who had played together as children were back together once more. Like the three musketeers, apart they might have been formidable, but together they were capable of swashbuckling their way to even greater heights of fame and fortune. As Gianni

admitted in *Signatures*, 'Donatella and Santo make me feel more complete, give a sense of continuity to my work. I sometimes see my mother in Donatella, my father in Santo. I am always the baby.' Having both his brother and sister now gathered around him obviously gave Gianni a strong sense of security in the rather insecure world of fashion.

Professionally, Donatella's contribution was (and is) enormous, although she prefers to play down her role. At first, she was merely Gianni's muse — he called her his 'perfect woman' — but gradually, he allowed her more input into the collections and the woman who once said 'less is less as far as I'm concerned' grasped the opportunity with both beautifully-manicured hands. The result of their collaboration — 'we complement each other,' he once said — is the style that we now know and can easily recognize as Versace — bold, exuberant, walking a fine line (and sometimes falling off it) between glamour and downright flashiness. As Susannah Barron wrote in the *Guardian* newspaper after his death, 'You could never accuse him of understatement.'

In Versace's last haute couture collection, shown in Paris in July 1997, he had begun to move away from flash-trash. His style was similar to that of his early collections. Was he stung by accusations of vulgarity, or had he simply gone as far as he could go? We will never know. However, when we think of Versace, we don't think of conservative little suits in twelve shades of beige — that's Giorgio Armani's territory — instead we think of big, bold and brashly printed shirts, heavily beaded eveningwear and gold — lots of it. He is a fashion icon precisely because we can all conjure up a distinct image of his clothes so easily.

The quintessential Versace look was forged after Donatella's arrival, principally in the key 1991–93 period. To watch a Versace catwalk show in the early 1990s was to witness a parade of colour and sparkle, the like of which would have made a Las Vegas showgirl blush. Print piled upon print and then embroidery and beading was added on top. It was an assault on the senses.

'Excess is entertaining, eccentricity stimulating. Only one rule applies, spontaneity,' Versace wrote in *Signatures*. Aided and abetted by Donatella, he applied this ethos with the enthusiasm of a lottery winner. Greco–Roman details were mixed with elements of cubist art, bright Baroque prints were applied to leggings and his trademark Medusa head sprouted on everything, from shoes to handbags, to the buttons on a leather jacket or a denim ballgown.

Versace was the first designer to use denim in a couture collection. In 1990, he put jeans on his Atelier catwalk. The French fashion establishment were predictably appalled. But Coco Chanel fashioned little suits from the sort of jersey used for men's underwear and that caused a stir too. Today, Coco's cardigan suit is a staple of every woman's wardrobe, whether stitched by Chanel seamstresses or run up in millions by a mass-market chain store. Versace's clothes may have been expensive, but at heart he was a populist. The layers of print and glitter were easily understandable by those who didn't 'get' Jil Sander or Yohji Yamamoto, which is why it is Versace who has continually been so comprehensively copied around the world.

The Aladdin's cave effect of Versace at his most flamboyant in the early 1990s could be over-powering. What drove him to such excess? Again, we need to remember the times. Britain may have already been in recession by 1991, but Europe and the USA continued to prosper and, like the last revellers at a New Year's Eve party, these markets were doing a drunken conga well after other, wiser souls had retired, hungover, to bed. Versace provided the perfect wardrobe for lovers of conspicuous consumption. Yes, the style was garish and yes, it was over-the-top, but when every

shop assistant and office tea boy was sporting a fake Rolex watch, Gianni's style was simply a step on from that. 'He knew us better than we knew ourselves. He understood the basic human need to show off. Through his work, he made a unique statement which, in a phrase, was that bad taste is much cooler than good taste if you push it far enough,' fashion historian Colin McDowell wrote in the *Sunday Times*. Yet, if Versace had been merely a clever stylist, a whizz with fancy buttons and bows, he could not have conquered the world of fashion. The surface detailing may have caught the eye, but it was the silhouette that sold the dress.

'Versace woman has no interest in being a lady. She knows that babes have more fun,' continued McDowell. And, indeed, the babe, in something beaded and plunging, is the enduring Versace image. 'Versace wasn't a revolutionary,' explains Vicki Woods. 'His progression was in things like technique, not in cut. His clothes were quite traditional. They curve out at the

Gianni and his 'perfect woman', Donatella – with suntan, but without make-up?

bosom, in at the waist and out again over the hips.' This made for some great pictures on a catwalk, but it also caused criticism from some quarters with the vampish silhouette being interpreted as cartoonish misogyny. 'A gay man designing for women – well, what do you expect?' asked some. However, this is too lazy an accusation. Many female designers, Vivienne Westwood among them, have a following among gay men. Orders for Westwood's women's platform shoes routinely arrive requesting sizes eight, nine and ten. To the development of Gianni's torch singer style, his sexuality was probably less important than his proximity to Donatella. In her, he had a ready-made model and muse who was eager to sport ever more outrageously female designs. Besides, as Woods says, 'Before Versace, there was Alma Cogan and she had to get her clothes from somewhere.'

The idea that Versace designed only for an ideal of womanhood is another myth that needs nailing. There aren't many American size fourteens hanging in a Versace boutique. The woman who can afford Gianni's clothes can also afford a personal trainer, liposuction and sashimi for breakfast, lunch and tea, but his garments always look best on someone who has a few curves. For a designer who designs for a boyish silhouette, it is necessary to glance in Giorgio Armani's direction, not Gianni Versace's. Sarah Walter, Fashion Director of British *Marie Claire* magazine, explains, 'Versace's stuff looks better on a good body, a womanly body. Then it really comes to life. He made real women look damned fantastic.' And he made a lot of money in the process. GV

Building An Empire

ianni Versace was a gifted designer. However, talent alone does not build multi-million dollar empires. The fashion industry is littered with the lost dreams of promising couturiers. Neither nifty tricks with gold buttons, nor clever conceits with baroque-printed Lycra could have bankrolled Gianni's lavish lifestyle — the private jets, the fabulous palazzos, the Picassos and Schnabels, the intimate dinners for 200 and the glossy store openings, studded with both celebrities and the attendant paparazzi.

Conspiracy theorists have inevitably had a field day, both during Versace's life and since his death. Reports of personal relationships, even close friendships, with certain key Mafia figures dogged Versace during his lifetime. Given his background in Reggio de Calabria, an area so firmly in the grip of organized crime, at least a few of his boyhood friends would inevitably have ended up working for the Mob. Then there is the manner of his death. Early police reports described Versace's murderer as being 'dressed like a tourist'. 'Isn't that the way Mafia hitmen operate?', some asked. The fact that the two bullets which killed him were delivered at point blank range to the back of his head and, if some onlookers are to be believed, a dead sparrow was placed next to the body, merely polished the theory that he was the victim of execution by the *Cosa Nostra*.

But personal friendship and professional involvement are two entirely different things. A fashion insider, who prefers not to be named, says, 'Versace enjoyed the whole macho thing of being seen with these people, partying with them, but another part of him resisted letting them get involved in his business.' The Versace family have always vehemently denied any professional relationship with organized crime. In 1994 they successfully sued the British *Independent on Sunday* newspaper and secured a significant out-of-court settlement after it was wrongly suggested that Mafia money was being laundered through the Versace group.

There is no doubt that Versace grew rapidly. From one small store on Milan's Via della Spiga in 1978, the company now boasts over 300 boutiques in every major capital in the world. And not just any boutiques. Before the London store on swish Old Bond Street opened its doors in 1991, Versace spent £11 million on its

transformation from a bank into a stupendously lavish retailing environment. 700 square metres of Brocatello marble were laid and bronze pillars and balustrades were decorated with a kilo of gold leaf. Had Versace lined the walls with chunks of The Elgin Marbles and placed Tutankhamun's mummy in a corner of one of the changing rooms, they would not have looked out of place.

So how did he do it? How did a boy from a not particularly nice part of Southern Italy, one without wealthy parents or much of an education, make enough money to swathe his shops in gold and marble and to cover himself in all the trappings of a

Claudia models a duvet from Versace's home Signature line on the back of his book, Do Not Disturb *(Abbeville Press).*

In 1994 the ready-to-wear collections in Milan fell during the World Cup soccer tournament. While other designers fumed at the emptiness of their post-show soirées, invitées having adjourned to the nearest TV, Versace employed a clever ruse to ensure his glamorous party was full. He had a huge video screen erected on one side of the dance floor at his party so that revellers could catch the latest scores.

Football is for Football

millionaire lifestyle? Italy's tax system may have something to do with it. The government made a half-hearted stab at eradicating corruption with its much-vaunted *Mani Pulite* (clean hands) policy a couple of years ago. Mariuccia Mandelli, the woman behind the label Krizia, and Giorgio Armani both admitted to bribing the tax authorities with sums of around 100 million lire (or $65,000). They were fined, as was Gianfranco Ferre. However, it was Santo Versace who was punished most heavily. He admitted paying out in the region of $160,000 in bribes to obtain favourable audits and was given a fourteen-month suspended jail sentence. He immediately launched an appeal.

Outsiders may be appalled that such senior figures in a generally high-profile manufacturing industry could confess to bribery. But the affair hardly raised an eyebrow in Italy.

In a country where various governments have been repeatedly rocked by corruption scandals, a little oiling of the wheels is accepted business practice. *Mani Pulite* was an embarrassment, but nothing more. No collections were cancelled and none of the buyers were put off. Neither Giorgio Armani nor Gianni Versace felt the need to hide themselves away in shame. Indeed, at the collections that followed the affair they, along with Gianfranco Ferre and Mariuccia Mandelli, took to the catwalk as normal. It was merely as if Claudia Schiffer had chipped her nail polish back stage.

Italian tax laws are extra-ordinarily lax. Those who point to Calvin Klein or Ralph Lauren, both of whom have taken a long time to build comparable empires, and question how Versace could have achieved his success so quickly, should remember that American tax regulations are quite stringent. It is not inconceivable that an Italian company with a whole network of international outposts (boutiques, for example) could employ a team of accountants who were clever enough to legally shuffle money around and could end up paying almost no tax at all. Because Versace spA is a privately owned company (a flotation on the Tokyo, New York and London stock exchanges planned for autumn 1997 was put on hold following Gianni's death), this means that full disclosure of company accounts is not mandatory.

Still, to suggest that the Versace empire is one great conjuring trick is to under-estimate both the power and importance of the Versace label and the immense achievement this represents for the Versace family. Stop someone in the street, particularly a label-conscious teenager, and ask them to name half a dozen designers. Versace will almost certainly be on the list, if not the first upon it. Flick through the racks of a mass market store or leaf through the pages of a mail order catalogue and the Versace stamp will be somewhere — on one garment, if not hundreds. The Versace look, the one that has proved so influential, is not a mirage. It is real and the fact that the public recognizes it and other firms copy its ideas is a testament to the talent and sheer brute determination of Gianni, Santo and Donatella Versace . . .

When Santo joined his brother Gianni in Milan in 1976, he did so with a solid business background. The shyest of the siblings but also the most athletic — he played college basketball — Santo realized from the start that control was the key to success. 'To begin with, Versace decided to stay independent, becoming one of the few major labels in control of the entire fashion cycle, from design to retailing,' he wrote in the brochure that accompanied the launch of Versus in 1989. Rather than simply handing over responsibility for manufacturing to licensees, the family have retained a controlling interest in ten of its manufacturing licenses.

This desire for control is central to the characters and careers of the Versace triumvirate. It is a major factor, not only in the building of the company, but also in the polishing of the Versace enigma. To maintain control, they have chosen, wherever possible, to keep things in the family. Outsiders, although tolerated, are never completely trusted.

According to Fiammetta Rocco (the journalist who authored the I*ndependent on Sunday* article over which Versace sued), writing in British *Punch* magazine, an employee told her,

'They operate on a basis of terrorism, complete and utter terrorism. . . No-one who works there feels at ease. Ever. It is nightmarish.' This employee goes as far as to give the impression that working for Gianni Versace was tantamount to joining a religious cult — 'To prosper, you have to completely take on their mentality. Gianni wants everyone to think of him as some sort of living god.' she said. This may be a bit over the top, even if the stories of staff being showered with diamond jewellery are more than matched by others of employees being completely frozen out for an unwise comment or a careless criticism.

(*Below*) **Gianni turning Japanese; Origami coat** *Autumn/Winter 1984* (*Left*) **Dynasty checks** *Autumn/Winter 1986.*

The kind of lace gown Grandma definitely wouldn't wear
Autumn/Winter 1985.

Perhaps it's something to do with the artistic temperament, or maybe they are simply over-indulged by those around them, but fashion designers are notorious for being demanding bosses. They invariably run their personal empires in the manner of particularly fickle rulers of South American banana republics. Jean Muir, for example, banned her staff from eating oranges in the design studio because she disliked the smell. But there cannot be another manufacturing industry that is required to present a totally new product line, with all its attendant production and marketing problems, every six months. As Gianni admitted, he suffered from 'the big pressure'. Vicki Woods, 'It's the untenable mix of having to be flouncy creatures one second and ruthless captains of industry the next. They're all barking, these guys. But at least Gianni was cheerful.'

The desire for control was an inevitable source of friction between the Versace siblings. During his lifetime, Gianni owned the most shares in the company — 45 per cent. The rest were split between Donatella, who was Vice President and Santo, who acted as Chief Executive. Santo was

supposed to be in sole charge of the financial side of the operation, a responsibility he wore heavily. Even so, Gianni was known to interfere. Epic rows between the two ensued, often over the telephone. Donatella was less likely to stay quiet. One fashion writer, who wants to remain anonymous, says, 'Santo has only one gear, neutral, while Donatella is on turbo.' Trudie Styler, a close friend of Donatella, once said of her, 'She says exactly what she damn well thinks.'

Disagreements between Donatella and Gianni, when they occurred, were of a creative, not a financial nature. Gianni told *Kaleidoscope* magazine, 'There's a great deal of critical freedom between us because I want the best for her, as she wants the best for me. We don't get drunk on mawkishness or things like that when we see a piece of clothing done by the other. I've never heard her say, 'Ah, that's divine.' This is our strength. There's a great deal of critical freedom between us.' Gianni and Donatella spoke up to twelve times a day by phone when they weren't together and he was still very much the elder brother. He told *Kaleidoscope*, 'Sometimes we ought to talk more together, because she [Donatella] tends towards the mono-look, whereas I prefer more variety.' Ouch!

Initially, Donatella was put in charge of accessories only.

However, the handbags weighed down with gilded embellishments and the shoes that sprouted any and every sort of printed and spangly decoration were clearly the work of someone who was aching to get her hands on a larger canvas. In 1989 Donatella got her chance with the launch of the diffusion line, Versus. Exactly how much of a free hand Donatella was given with Versus by Gianni is a matter of some debate. It was customary for Gianni and Donatella to take to the catwalk together at the end of a Versus fashion show and Gianni once said, 'I really do step in.' However, the exuberance of the range – low on simple white toga dresses and high on scarlet leather – suggests that it was (and still is) Donatella's baby.

It is the combination of Gianni's love of classicism and Donatella's taste for glamorous streetwise chic that is at the root of the Versace success story. As Gianni once commented, 'Donatella's strength is that she makes everything she touches something modern.' Shown in New York, Versus has always had a more trendy, urban hard edge. Of Versus, Donatella said, 'The strong image impact is never weakened, but finely tuned with a mediated sense of conservative chic.' Only Donatella could describe Versus as conservative. Gianni preferred to call Versus a 'young and vivacious line, which is never commonplace.' In reality,

Well, they said a Versace outfit could light up a room. Nude model with lampshade pictured in **Do Not Disturb** *(Abbeville Press).*

it is less for the ladies who lunch than their daughters who go clubbing, albeit at some rather upmarket nightspots.

Once Gianni had given Versus to Donatella, the professional relationship between brother and sister was not always comfortable. 'Sure, as he [Gianni] always repeats to me, it's necessary to know about the past and about history. But I'm lucky, he acts as my interpreter,' Donatella commented at the time of the Versus launch. Gianni promptly replied, 'She loves looking at what I do then translates it in her own way.' So who exactly was interpreting whom? The vision of Gianni scribbling adjustments to Donatella's Versus sketches and Donatella rubbing them out again swims into the imagination.

Gianni was keen to give the impression that he kept a firm hand on Donatella. This cannot have been just down to pride: it was also a smart marketing move. When Versus debuted, it was Gianni whose name was known and whose designs people wanted to buy. In much the same way that other designers employ rooms full of design 'assistants' who actually produce the vast majority of what then appears

(Above) **How to pad shoulders the Versace way**
Autumn/Winter 1987
(Right)
Architectural pleats
Autumn/Winter 1989.

Versace A-Z

As a teenager, Andrew Cunanan (the man that the FBI believe to have murdered Versace) attended the top-flight Bishop's School in La Jolla, a suburb of San Diego. He graduated in 1987. The yearbook records his election by his classmates as the student 'most likely not to be forgotten'.

Graduation
G is for Graduation

under the designer's name, a designer (however creatively profligate) can only crank out so many frock ideas in a season. Gianni definitely needed another pair of hands but commercially, he really needed to underplay Donatella's importance.

The fact that Gianni billed his sister as co-designer of Versus was, actually pretty generous. Still, she wasn't to get ideas above her station. 'I've nicknamed her Madame Chanel or Madame Schiaparelli, depending,' Gianni told *Kaleidoscope*. As there is not enough room for both a Madame Chanel and a Monsieur Versace in most design rooms, it's a wonder they only argued. Had they not been brother and sister, they would, one suspects, have been biting chunks out of each other on a daily basis.

Fortunately, the Versace empire expanded fast enough to offer outlets for the egos of both Gianni and Donatella.

Diversification is the other key plank in Santo's business strategy. Santo once explained it as an effort to construct the 'Versace's World'. The range of products available to those who wish to worship at the feet of fashion's last emperor is staggering. At the pinnacle of the Gianni Versace product pyramid is Atelier, his haute couture line, which he launched in 1989. At the time the French fashion establishment was most indignant that a mere Italian should have the gall to muscle in on their territory. They may have tolerated Gianfranco Ferre as designer-in-residence at the house of Dior and the German designer Karl Lagerfeld at Chanel,

(Above) **These boots are made for teetering** *Autumn/Winter 1994* *(Above right)* **This bag is made for lunching** *Autumn/Winter 1994.*

but he had been around for so long that most people had forgotten that he wasn't born French. The fact he kept a residence in Monaco, that most *Paris Match* of locations, situated close enough to Princesses Caroline and Stephanie that he could pop round with a cup of sugar or suitcase of evening gowns, helped too.

But Versace was Italian to the core. Unlike Christian Lacroix, then a new and much celebrated entrant to the couture scene, Versace was not adept at the sort of frou-frou milkmaid outfits that go down such a storm with creaky Gallic matriarchs. His collections were sexy and showy, as was his mode of presenting them. After a launch soirée at the Gare d'Orsay, attended by Madame Mitterand, Versace chose the Ritz hotel as his regular Atelier show venue. As well as being the home for many years of Versace's great heroine Coco Chanel, the Ritz is the most ostentatious of all Paris's grand hotels. He also secured himself a slot right at the start of the couture collections schedule, thereby stealing a march on his new rivals.

Atelier produces exclusive one-off creations. When made to order, an Atelier evening gown can easily top $30,000. But then, as the saying goes, 'If you have to ask the price, you can't afford it.'

Who said leggings couldn't be hip?
Marpessa models a beaded Marilyn pair
Autumn/Winter 1990.

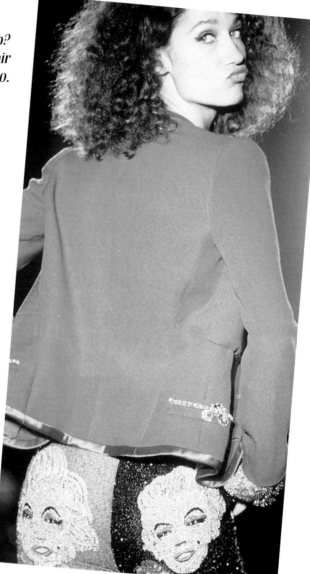

For mere mortals, next down in the Versace product pyramid are his ready-to-wear main lines that are shown in Milan. Although not exactly in the 'I-like-it-but-I-can't-decide-whether-to-get-it-in-the-red-or-the-blue-I-better-have-both' price bracket (unless you're Elton John, in which case you take the purple, green, orange and pink as well), main line Versace is more affordable. Ticket prices for a suit are in the hundreds rather than the thousands of dollars.

From the start, Gianni Versace presented both women's and men's collections. The design ethos is similar, if necessarily more muted in the men's line, although not that muted. 'I don't know who buys the men's line except Sylvester Stallone,' says David Hayes, freelance stylist and former Fashion Editor of British *Today* newspaper. 'Even a simple black suit always has something of the David Copperfield about it.' The bright colours and detailing which veers towards either Las Vegas cowboy or Cuban pimp means that it is, if not quite an acquired taste, aimed at a niche market. 'It's too camp to be gay. It works if you're a six foot two rugby player,' explains Hayes. The fact that Versace's macho minder Bruno always looks so fabulous in his black Versace suit is the proof of that statement.

To the core men's and women's lines, the Versace group added lingerie, beachwear and childrenswear. Yes, your *bambino* can wear gold too! Moving a little cheaper (relatively speaking), we reach the Versace diffusion lines — Versus, Istante, Versace Jeans Couture, Signature, Versace Sport, Versatile and Versace Classic V2. If only a few pop stars, movie starlets and socialites wear Atelier, the Versace diffusion lines sell by the bucket load. Everyone, from American Midwest dairy queens, squeezing themselves into a pair of Versace 'Jeans Couture' denims that are a size too small, to streetwise kids buying tee-shirts three sizes too big, wants (it seems) to sport the Versace logo. At the bottom of the pyramid we

Versace main line handbag will be different (and more expensive) from one sold as Istante. Organizing these goods into separate collections has the benefit of extending the product line, and therefore the sales potential, while not tarnishing the image of items at the top end of the Versace range. That Istante handbag may be cheaper, but the main line Versace one is still rather special.

But it doesn't end there. Running in tandem with the clothing ranges is the Versace 'Home Signatures' collection. This

'It's the untenable mix of having to be flouncy creatures one second and ruthless captains of industry the next. They're all barking.'

Vicki Woods, Contributing Editor, American *Vogue*

have all the add-ons — jewellery (real and costume), perfumes, bags, belts, shoes, ties, scarves, gloves, hats, sunglasses and, most recently, cosmetics. All of these are duplicated at different price points and marketed as separate collections. For example, a

encompasses everything from china, glass, quilts and cushions, vases, picture frames, lamps and tiles to furnishing fabrics, beds, tables and bath linen. Those who can't get enough of Versace by simply wearing it can now furnish an entire home with Versace

Versace A-Z

Despite their many fabulous palazzos around the world, there are times when the Versace family find themselves in unfamiliar surroundings. One such occasion occurred in Paris in July 1997, shortly before Versace's death. Donatella was overseeing the creation of a new advertising campaign by photographer Mario Testino. Two studios were hired. Before shooting could begin in the first studio, a truckload of Versace furniture, rugs and *objets d'art* had to be carried up the stairs and arranged in the second so as to create a luxurious and relaxing home-from-home for Donatella.

H is for Home From Home

items. Each morning, the Versace addict could pull back the Versace sheets on their bed, walk across a Versace rug to draw their Versace curtains, take a bath and pat themselves dry with a Versace towel before breakfasting off Versace china while their Versace-slippered feet rest upon a Versace-tiled kitchen floor.

Similar marketing models are employed by all the big designer names. Ralph Lauren, for example, has his famous polo player logo stamped across everything from velvet evening jackets to pillowcases. The standard line offered by designers for this rampant cashing-in on

their name is that it makes their goods available to a wider range of people. Out of the goodness of the fashion maestro's heart, we are told, even the most impoverished consumer can sample the luxury of owning a famous label. However, the democratizing of fashion is also a pretty good excuse for making a lot of money. In 1996 the Versace group achieved sales of $560 million for clothing, accessories made $250 million and housewares $40 million. The Versace fragrances — Blonde (named in honour of Donatella), The Dreamer, Blue Jeans and Versace L'Homme — reached sales of $150 million. Worldwide sales of Versace products are on course to top $1 billion this year.

As the mixed financial fortunes, historically speaking, of other big names such as Calvin Klein and Gucci demonstrate, attempting to build a fashion empire is like building a house of cards. It is a flimsy construction. There are two prerequisites for preventing its collapse. The first is that the most expensive items at the top of the product pyramid are genuinely desirable. They must have an aura of luxury that will rub off on the cheaper tee-shirts, bags, jewellery, etc. This is not just about attaching an enormous price tag (although that would impress a certain customer), but about making them really desirable. 'I remember borrowing a blouse. It cost $1500. It was a case of "think of a price and triple it". But it was beautifully made,' says David Hayes. Sarah Walter, Fashion Director of British *Marie Claire* magazine makes a similar point, 'His stuff is expensive, but it is fabulously well-made.'

If the quality is good, the next factor is a look that can transfer from premium to mass-market lines. A strong signature is not enough of a qualification for this. A John Galliano frock, for example, is easily identifiable, but the appeal of his style lies largely in his use of exquisite fabrics and ingenious cutting, both of which are ruinously expensive. 'Diffusing' Galliano, replicating his style in cheaper fabrics and doing away with the wasteful bias-cutting, is difficult. The powers that be at Dior, who have hired the English *enfant terrible*, will have an uphill struggle in trying to make any cheaper line work.

Versace, on the other hand, created a look that was not about silhouette but about surface detailing. 'He had very recognizable design features,' explains Annalisa Barbieri, Contributing Editor to Britain's *Independent on Sunday* newspaper. 'In the fashion business, we can recognize a Helmut Lang dress. But you don't have to be in the fashion business to recognize Versace'. The Versace look — the scarf prints, the gold fiddly bits — could as well be applied to a $30,000 evening gown as it could to a $30 ashtray.

Indeed, the homeware collection is perhaps the most

pure example of Versace chic. As Sarah Walter says, 'It is ostentatious and showy and much more of a label than his clothes. You could put on his clothes with something else and change it, but a tea cup or a cushion – no-one can change it.'

Gianni Versace once described his style as 'uncontrolled by rules' and there was an apparent anarchy about his mixing of leather and lace, fur and sequins, ancient and modern. However, there was method in his apparent madness. 'He realized before anyone else that the meritocratic society of the 1990s needed to be mirrored by our clothing – and that is what he gave us, in colours and patterns that made most designers faint clean away at the boldness of it all,' fashion historian Colin McDowell wrote in the *Sunday Times*.

Figures for sales of counterfeit Versace goods are necessarily vague. Still, if you add in all the Versace-influenced and Versace-style garments that have been sold worldwide over the last five years, it must run into millions of dollars. 'There was a point at the beginning of the Nineties when you couldn't walk into a store

without seeing those bright shirts and leggings with some dreadful print snaking up the leg', says Grace Bradberry, of the London *Times* newspaper. The fact that the public queued up to buy these revolting items is, according to Bradberry, 'because we all wanted designer everything. And that meant Versace.' Versace had come to embody the whole designer era. How did he manage to do that? Enter, stage left: Linda, Naomi and Claudia. Ⓥ

A Versace leather boy
Autumn/Winter 1997.

Making Models Super

The year is 1991 and the place is Milan. On the second floor of an anonymous exhibition hall, a taxi ride away from the city's glamorous shopping district but a world away in terms of aura, Gianni Versace is holding his autumn/winter ready-to-wear fashion show. The drab interior is dimly lit, but for a gleaming, marble-covered catwalk that has been constructed down the centre of the room. Sitting at about shoulder height — it is ten feet wide and forty to fifty feet long — while not quite capacious enough to land a private jet, it is more than adequate for a brace of polo ponies to gallop up and down . . .

Ranged around the catwalk in a long U-shape are rows of gilded chairs. These are jammed together and each one has a little card taped to the back. The chairs that are positioned along the front row, a foot or so away from the catwalk, are inscribed with a name which has been written as elegantly as you can in magic marker. To the left are the names of VIP press — Suzy Menkes of *International Herald Tribune*, Anna Wintour of American *Vogue*, John Fairchild of *Women's Wear Daily*. To the right are the VIP buyers — Bergdorf Goodman, Nieman Marcus, Harrods, etc. These are the guests whose pages or store

Quintessential supermodel moments; (Above) Linda, Cindy, Naomi & Christy take to the catwalk March 1991 (Left) Gianni and his most fervent fans Christy, (left) and Linda (right).

windows are coveted and whose reviews and order books are feared. Other front row chairs simply have a large and tantalizing 'reserved' written on them and these are for celebrities.

From the second row back, there are no names, just cards with letters and numbers written on them. These correspond to those scribbled in the corner of thick card invitations clutched by the crowd that is milling about. This seating system is similar to that which might be employed by the United Nations for what promises to be a particularly volatile meeting. Nationalities are organized in blocks. All the French are seated together with an invisible wall dividing them from the British, the Germans and the Japanese. Should a stray German wander into British territory, his or her presence is greeted with suspicion, if not downright outrage. You can't put your designer beachtowel here, Fraulein.

The only place where *entente cordiale* is evident is in the section of seating at the centre of the U-shape. This is the international VIP area. It offers the best view, directly down the runway to the back wall, which is decorated with 'Gianni Versace' in giant letters. Special friends, be they press, buyers or rock stars, secure one of these seats. The downside of sitting here is having the massed ranks of photographers directly behind you. Any pretensions towards gentility are punctured by the shouted comments of the long lense merchants — 'Linda! Naomi! turn around!'. Sometimes the comments are more colourful. As the crowd shuffles in — any faster movement is rendered impossible by the combination of tight security at the entrance and a lot of stilettos — anticipation is mixed with heavy designer scent. And the distinct aroma of sweat. It is hot, very hot — too many bodies, not enough oxygen. The Versace-dressed audience may only now be arriving, fifteen minutes before curtain up but the photographers have been crushed together, waiting, for anything up to two hours. Piled up on chairs, ladders and silver metal camera

Versace A-Z

In his book *Signatures,* Versace tried to trace the origins of his approach to design. 'Perhaps it was in my mother's dressmaker's shop when she tried a black dress on Mrs Ippoliti. A black dress is my earliest memory,' he wrote. 'In reality, that fitting has never ended.'

Ippoliti

is for Mrs Ippoliti

boxes, forty or fifty of them are packed into a space in which you couldn't swing a gold-embossed handbag. They are fractious. Occasionally, arguments break out in a mixture of French, Italian and English as one shifts an elbow a millimetre to the left or right and blocks another's lense. Suddenly the lights go down and there is a last minute scuffle as stragglers take their seats. Then, to a booming rock soundtrack, the show begins. No model will ever look as beautiful as on this runway. A mixture of superb lighting, including much use of backlight to give a halo effect, and exquisite make-up and hair renders even the most averagely

attractive mannequin into a goddess. Not that there are any average-looking women on Versace's catwalk. It is wall-to-wall Supermodels. Naomi, Cindy, Linda, Christy, Tatiana . . . they come tumbling towards the audience in a never-ending stream of gorgeousness. Sash-aying, preening, flirting with the cameras, they look like a genetic experiment to create an Amazonian super-race.

Just when sensory overload threatens, the lights go out. There is a pause. The soundtrack switches to George Michael. Four figures appear at the other end of the catwalk, wearing mini-length toga dresses in pastel chiffon and with their arms round each other's tiny waists. They are Linda, Cindy, Naomi and Christy and, as they saunter, their long limbs stretch out ahead of them in perfect time with each other. They get to the end of the catwalk and stop, giggling and miming the words of the record. Four of the most famous women in the world, the ones who don't get out of bed for less than $10,000, whose faces adorn the covers of every magazine and whose bodies are spread across billboards in every city in the world, are standing, luxuriating in their own fabulousness. Forty flashguns threaten to spontaneously combust.

That moment in 1991 provided the quintessential image of Supermodeldom. Glamour, money, beauty — it all summed up everything that these remarkable creatures called 'Supermodels' had come to represent. It couldn't have happened on any other catwalk but Versace's. And, as Hilary Alexander wrote just after Versace's death, 'He virtually single-handedly invented the Supermodel.'

There were models before Versace, even famous ones. From

Twiggy in the 1960s to Marie Helvin and Jerry Hall in the 1970s, these were women whose faces were well-known and whose lifestyles were picked over in newspaper society columns. Still, their fame was largely by association. They had to date a famous man, preferably a rock star, to be seen to really make it big — Jerry Hall and Bryan Ferry, Jerry Hall and Mick Jagger, etc. etc. It was Versace who gave

Naomi goes Flamenco five years before Joaquim
Autumn/Winter 1992.

(Above) **Helena does designer bondage**
Autumn/ Winter 1992
(Left) **Linda as the rhinestone cowgirl**
Autumn/Winter 1992.

catwalk queens fame in their own right. Sure, Cindy got hitched to Richard Gere, but if she benefited from his Hollywood connections, his profile was raised just as much by her fame.

When Versace came on the scene, catwalk models were a distinct breed. In the way that actors are often divided into those who 'tread the boards' (stick to the stage) and those who prefer to perform in front of a camera, models either did magazine or runway work. They rarely did both. Magazine or 'editorial' girls were regarded as too fat — we are talking relatively here — to look good on a catwalk. Runway models are expected to have a skeletal frame that belies the consumption of a square meal in the recent or even distant past. Magazine models also didn't know how to 'walk'. The right runway 'walk' is part cheetah, part astronaut — the hips are shunted forward, the shoulders back and the neck extended. A good catwalk model, the type who could undo the most fiddly buttons on a jacket, slip it to fall

halfway down her shoulders, while turning on one high heel, could work well into her thirties, an age when she wouldn't be employed to sweep the floor on a magazine photo-shoot.

What Versace did was to break down the barrier that existed between editorial and runway. He took the hottest magazine models and put them on his catwalk. Maybe some of them didn't walk too well — Claudia Schiffer never quite eradicated the *bier keller* bounce from her runway performances — but their faces were pure magic in the long lenses. And this was the point. Versace wanted to sell clothes, but not necessarily those on the catwalk. As he built his empire, he had watches, bags and tea cups to sell. All that he needed was publicity and, of course, the Supermodels delivered it.

Traditional catwalk models might have been able to show clothes off to best advantage, but they were ingenues when it came to flirting with a camera. With Claudia, Christy, Cindy *et al.*,

every picture was a *Vogue* cover.

The photographers, and newspaper and magazine picture desks for whom they worked, loved it. 'By using Supermodels, Versace helped newspapers and TV accept fashion,' explains David Hayes, freelance stylist and former Fashion Editor of British *Today* newspaper. Instead of being presented with snaps of some bony old creature swinging a pleated shawl elegantly, here were pictures of young, sexy girls falling out of plunging evening gowns. 'There was always that moment with Stephanie Seymour when you definitely got the feeling that her top was much too tight for her breasts,' says catwalk photographer Christopher Moore.

It was a happy coincidence for Versace that his discovery of the Supermodels coincided with the explosion of colour printing, particularly in the British media. Newspapers and magazines were looking for eye-catching pictures and Helena Christensen in sequins fitted the bill. That these sequins invariably came in the sort of colours capable of bonding the retina to the back of the eyeball increased their attraction for the

Gianni as supermodel Svengali. This group includes Naomi, Carla, Yasmeen, Eva and Kristen.

'He single-handedly invented the Supermodel.'

Hilary Alexander, Fashion Editor of the

British *Daily* and *Sunday Telegraph*

Cindy in a mini-crini,
Spring/Summer 1992.

(Above) **Why use one bead when you can use a truckload? Claudia dazzles**
Spring/ Summer 1992
(Top right) **Courting the press, Christy pleases the people at Vogue**
Spring/Summer 1991
(Right) **Carla outshines the opposition**
Spring/Summer 1992.

media still further. Why feature a beige Armani suit when you could show a scarlet Versace mini dress?

Still, it was the girls as much, if not more, than the clothes that everyone was looking at, at the beginning of the 1990s. They were just so startling and Versace made them even more so. 'It's ridiculous when people trumpet the fact that a garment worn by Claudia Schiffer is necessarily beautiful,' Versace was to comment at the time. 'A garment is beautiful if it's beautiful. It's ugly if it's ugly. Of course, it's the age-old discovery of boiling water. However, it seems to me that a lot of people still haven't discovered boiling water. The result is they make the most beautiful models ugly.'

While other designers forced models to adopt a totally new look each season, including weird make-up and a bizarre hairstyle, Versace never made his mannequins look ridiculous. Instead, he polished their own individual charisma and glamour so that, like film stars of the 1930s, 1940s and 1950s, whatever role his models were asked to play, they always played themselves.

Marilyn Monroe is always Marilyn Monroe in whichever movie she appears. That is what made her a star, rather than just an actress. Claudia Schiffer is always Claudia Schiffer, whatever she wears and that's what makes her a true Supermodel.

And the wardrobe helped, of course . . . 'Impressive,' is how Vicki Woods describes the whole Versace catwalk effect. 'On a very young girl with lots of blonde hair and lots of cleavage hanging out [who could she mean?] it could be tarty, but really this was just very, very female clothing,' she says. Versace's only rule was to flatter the faces and figures of his models and to make them look sexy with a capital 'S'. 'Those girls are like clothes pegs and he bosoms them,' says Woods. Christopher Moore agrees. 'Cindy Crawford always looked wonderful in Versace. She looked brilliant,' he adds.

If Cindy Crawford's pneumatic curves looked made to wear Versace, others seemed less well-

Versace A-Z

Versace always kept his eye on young designers, not simply as potential rivals, but also as possible protégés. When American Marc Jacobs stopped designing for the Perry Ellis label in New York and launched his own line, Versace made a point of attending his first show. It was a rare honour and a major boost for a fashion fledgling.

J is for Jacobs

suited. There was a point in 1992–3 when the Superwaif threatened to kill off the Supermodel.

Skinny girls, with shiny, unmade-up faces like Kate Moss, had arrived with a new, dressed down anti-glamour attitude. They represented everything that Versace wasn't.

But it is a testament to Versace's skill that he managed to incorporate them, almost seamlessly, into his standard line-up. Alexandra Shulman, Editor of British *Vogue*, says, 'He always moved on. He always had a take on what was going on. He used the new girls, Emma Balfour, Kate, Stella . . . All the new girls were in his show immediately, but he made them into Versace girls.'

This was no mean task. Vicki Woods recounts the tale of watching Kate Moss undergoing a Valentino fitting. 'Helena Christensen was there, twirling about in something pink and fabulous,' she explains. When Woods watched the show, Kate Moss was absent.

'I asked Carlos [Valentino's PR] why, and he said I should ask Valentino. He said his clothes didn't work on her.'

But Kate did appear in the same season on Versace's catwalk. 'It was bloody well impressive that he could take Claudia, with yards of blonde hair, and also take someone of smaller build like Kate and size it down and it worked,' says Woods.

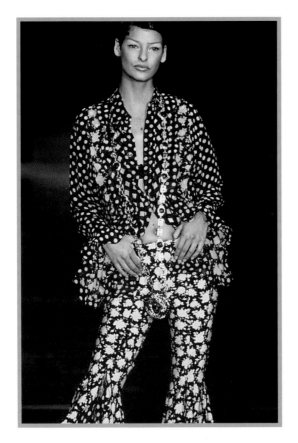

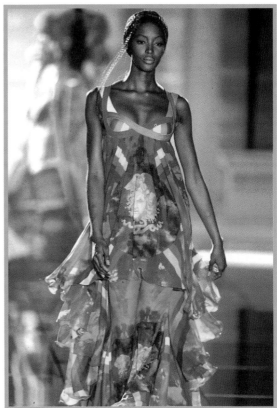

(Left) **Marpessa looking cute**
Spring/Summer 1993
(Above) **Linda in medallion man chic**
Spring/Summer 1993
(Above right) **Naomi in bias-cut frilly**
Spring/Summer 1993.

Versace A-Z

Versace's love of kitsch was central to his design philosophy. It's what separates him from his great rival, Armani. Only a man with a sophisticated appreciation of good bad taste could have created outfits that outrageously mixed mock leopard, zebra and crocodile all at once, or fashioned a beaded catsuit from multiple Andy Warhol-esque Marilyn Monroe faces.

K is for Kitsch

The inevitable effect of Versace's hyping of the Supermodel was that they upstaged the clothes. No garment, however outrageous, could compete with Christy Turlington on a really good day. Still, by the early 1990s, Versace had rewritten the catwalk show manual and there was no going back. Designers who tried to swim against the Supermodel tide just ended up looking wet. 'It was the complete antithesis of Armani. He felt his clothes should speak for themselves,' says David Hayes. In the end, even Armani had a stab at putting Supermodels on his runway, although Kate Moss looked decidedly uncomfortable.

Other designers looked at Versace and were quite appalled. Some of them even believed that he was buying his way to the top. 'At the end of the Eighties he [Versace] wasn't taken very seriously, but they couldn't ignore him because of the amount of publicity he was generating,' says David Hayes. 'The Supermodels gave his clothes that stamp of approval, a sort of credibility.

Basically, he was buying respectability.' And how he bought . . . The famous $10,000 a day quote from Linda Evangelista couldn't have happened without Versace.

Precise figures on the financial inducements that Versace offered his favourite models are shrouded in secrecy. However, according to Hayes, 'he paid them enormous amounts of money. It was rumoured to be up to $200,000 a show.' And he paid this kind of money for not one or two Supermodels, but the entire pack. When Christy Turlington was said to have been given $80,000 to appear exclusively on Versace's runway, Versace's rivals realized that they were being priced out of the market. They got together to try to set a standard rate of pay for models. They decided that no one designer should have an exclusive on a model, but that the big names should appear in no more than ten shows each . . .

The fees paid to Supermodels polished their image and also that of Versace. He was the man with the golden cheque book. Now it was time to apply his touch to other icons. **GV**

'By using Supermodels, Versace helped newspapers and TV accept fashion'

David Hayes, freelance stylist

Versace A-Z

Versace's life was insured for a reported £13 million under a 'key man' policy at Lloyds of London. According to Charles Boyd, underwriter with the Kiln agency (the company heading the underwriters taking on the risk), the policy had been in place for 'several years and would probably cover murder.'

Lloyds

L is for Lloyds of London

Famous Friends, Famous Frocks

By the early 1990s, Gianni Versace was king of the catwalk. With the biggest models and the brashest clothes he had, quite simply, blown the opposition out of the water. OK, so Armani might have shifted more stock to the buyers but when it came to witnessing a spectacle of utter, jaw-dropping glamour, it was Gianni and not Giorgio for whom the crowds queued. Versace's were the hottest tickets in town(s). Even those who hated his clothes had to have one. As a result, the spectacle outside a Versace show was often as remarkable as the one inside.

On one memorable occasion, the Milanese fire brigade refused to allow any more people inside for fear of blocking the emergency exits. There was almost a near riot, as the fashion pack hitched up their minis and clambered in their Manolo Blahnik shoes over crash barriers. Security was brushed aside as the label-clad hoards surged forwards. Nothing, not fire, pestilence or plague, could have prevented the international style coterie from getting inside. Why the hysteria? Well, apart from the opportunity to view Linda, Kate and Christy in ritzy bondage gear up close and personal, there was the *Hello!* magazine factor.

If Versace's first masterstroke was to secure the services of the most famous faces and figures on the catwalk, his second was to woo celebrities into lining it. The buzz before a Versace show would go on for days. Would Sylvester Stallone be there? And what about Demi Moore? Was Elton John in town, and if so, what kind of hairstyle was he modelling this season? If and when Sly, Demi or Elton did turn up, they would be ushered in by Donatella, plus a battery of burly minders hired to fend off eager paparazzi, to a front row seat. From this commanding position they would study the drape of a waterfall-backed evening gown while everyone else simultaneously examined them for signs of cosmetic surgery.

Celebrity endorsements were a central part of Versace's marketing strategy. As Hilary Alexander wrote: 'He blended fame and fashion like a pop alchemist. His was a magic brew of hype and hysteria within which fashion flourished.'

Pictures of Supermodels walking down a catwalk are all very well, but they only fill newspapers and magazines four times a year (January and July Paris couture, March and October Milan and Paris ready-to-wear). Celebrities not only add further

hype at show time but they can also put a designer's creations in the news for fifty-two weeks of the year. The Oscars, Cannes, Montreux Rock Festival — there is always an occasion that demands a dramatic entrance and Versace was determined that that entrance should be made in one of his frocks.

'He [Versace] was very clever. He understood pop culture and how important it was to get a designer's name across to as many people as possible and if that meant having rock stars at your shows, fine,' says Alexandra Shulman.

'I see you in sequins, Eddy'. Gianni and HRH Prince Edward, 1991.

Rock stars, movie actresses, television personalities or those who were just famous for being famous — Wonderbra model Caprice being a case in point — were all grist to the Versace publicity mill. They stamped his name across the consciousness of the public, raising the profile of the Versace brand and giving it a glamour and a certain cachet which sent the cash tills ringing. Hamish Bowles, American *Vogue's* Editor-at-Large, told *Time* magazine: 'Versace moved fashion into the public arena in the most strident way.'

Alexandra Shulman says of Versace: 'He understood that people are prepared to pay a lot to be very noticeable and very high profile.' The question is, of course, how many of the stars Versace dressed actually paid for their finery? The fact that Demi Moore is never seen in the same glamorous gown twice suggests that either she's got a wardrobe the size of Wisconsin, or else the frocks go straight back to the press office the morning after.

All designers use celebrities. Even the snootiest fashion house operates like a public lending library, booking out $30,000 frocks like the latest Harold Robbins or Jackie Collins novel. Mr or Mrs Average might get short shrift if they asked Donna Karan, Calvin Klein or Gianfranco Ferre if they could borrow a dress for a special occasion, but for stars, that designer door is always open. 'You'd like a little something for a film premiére? Of course. We'll send a selection right over,' is the refrain echoing from press offices around the world, from Paris to Palm Springs.

But if all designers do it, Versace did it better than anyone else. Sarah Walter, Fashion Director of British *Marie Claire* magazine explains, 'He was the master of befriending people who were going to be photographed and making sure they were photographed in his kit.' In a way, Versace really had no other choice. It was the only ace that he had up his sleeve. Alexandra Shulman says, 'Versace used it more than Karl [Lagerfeld]. But then Karl had Chanel. He already had a whole other thing, an established house which was loaded with identity. Versace had to build a name from scratch.'

Versace A-Z

Seventy-seven year-old Monsignor Luciano Migliavacca conducted the memorial mass for Gianni Versace in the Duomo in Milan. When informed by the Versace family that Sting and Elton John were to sing the twenty-third Psalm during the service, the Monsignor refused to allow it, unless they auditioned for him first. 'Certainly, I knew their names, but it is necessary to be sure their voices were worthy of a solemn celebration of the mass,' Migliavacca explained. Elton and Sting gave a fifteen-minute private and unaccompanied performance of *The Lord is My Shepherd* for the Monsignor. 'They weren't perfect, but I'd have them back,' Migliavacca said after the service.

M is for Migliavacca

It is ironic that it was Armani, the man who ended up being so comprehensively upstaged by Versace, who first spotted the potential of stroking Hollywood egos by establishing a press office in Los Angeles. The Oscars were Armani territory long before Versace moved in. However, if names such as Jodi Foster and Eric Clapton have remained loyal to Armani —Clapton briefly flirted with Versace before defecting back again to Armani, causing farcical scenes involving stand-offs between rival Armani and Versace wardrobe departments on his joint tour with Elton John in 1992 — many more were successfully and permanently wooed by Versace.

The list of stars who have worn Versace reads like a *Who's Who* of the rich and famous. Julie Andrews, Barbara Bach, Kim Basinger, Jacqueline Bisset, David Bowie, Laura Dern, Bob Dylan, Rupert Everett, Bryan Ferry . . . the list snakes on through the celebrity alphabet right through to Italian singing sensation Zuchero. And Versace wasn't fussy about what field it was that his celebrities glittered in, just so long as they glittered. In *Men Without Ties* he wrote. 'I admire men who have the courage to become heroes.' His clothes horses were just as likely to be those who could balance a football as those who wore a grand tiara.

The fact that celebrities queued up to wear Versace is, in part, because his clothes were so Hollywood, even before a star put them on. The Versace style is glamorous, showy and ostentatious.

As Vicki Woods says, 'All that leather and S & M could be over the top. You couldn't go out to dinner in it, but you weren't

It's playfully classy and immediately rich.' In other words, it screams 'Look at me!' And, if you are a celebrity that's exactly what you want, even if you have just given an interview to the press in which you sincerely describe yourself as 'essentially a private person'.

For major, stadium-filling rock stars such as Elton John, Sting, Bruce Springsteen, Rod Stewart and Eric Clapton, the Versace look

" [Versace] understood that people are prepared to pay a lot to be very noticeable and very high profile."

Alexandra Shulman, editor British *Vogue*

meant to.' Well, not unless you were as famous as Demi Moore and the restaurant was Le Cirque, perhaps.

Versace's are clothes for film premiéres and glitzy charity bashes. kd lang wrote in *Rock and Royalty*: 'Versace fashion is elaborate, colourful and strong.

is particularly apt. 'Wearing Versace is like driving a Ferrari 70mph with the top down and the radio blasting. They are both fast, loud and grip every curve,' Elton John wrote in *Rock and Royalty*. Versace's clothing not only suits the rock sensibility, it also fits in with the

(Above) *Hollywood royalty in the shape of Liz Taylor comes to pay homage to Emperor Gianni.*

Versace's most famously royal client, Diana, the Princess of Wales. She would also meet a tragic death, and within weeks of Versace's own. The fashion world had so much to mourn in 1997.

lifestyle like a pair of Rod Stewart's 1970's leopard print trousers. 'I have to dress for an audience; they expect it. It is an essential part of my performance,' Elton John wrote. And, indeed, in the same way that the British Queen always wears bright colours in public so that her subjects can pick her out from a distance, so a Versace suit is made for wearing on the stage of a stadium rock concert. Even those who are four miles from the stage, have no trouble spotting Elton in fuchsia pink leather.

A Gianni Versace outfit has instant impact. To step out in one

Versace A-Z

Versace was a creature of habit. When in Miami, he liked to go out every morning and walk the few blocks to the Newscafé, and buy a magazine and coffee. Usually, he approached from the same direction, but Newscafé manageress Stephanie Vanover told *Time* magazine that on the day of his murder, Versace 'walked past the entrance, circled back round, then went in. It's almost as if he knew he was being followed.'

N is for Newscafé

is to upstage everyone else, as Liz Hurley found. When she attended the London premiére of her boyfriend Hugh Grant's movie *Four Weddings and a Funeral*, she was unknown. 'In that instance, the dress was probably more famous than her,' says Vicki Woods. Hurley's movie credits were sparse and those films in which she had appeared were strictly of the straight-to-video variety. Still, one night in *that* dress and she was a star, at least to the British tabloid newspaper world. From the moment her voluptuous curves were caught on camera, spilling from navy, safety-pinned crepe, her every move was breathlessly recorded. One ex-boyfriend was even persuaded to

reveal the secrets of their teenage relationship, resulting in the memorable headline in the British *Sun* newspaper: 'My Hurley Girlie Went Like A Steam Train'.

Such minor embarrassment, however, was far outweighed by the career boost that Versace's evening gown gave Ms Hurley. *That* frock turned out to be a gift from a fashion god. Hurley's new high profile may not have cut much ice with Joan Rivers — when introduced by Hugh to Liz at the Oscars, Joan said 'Who?' — but it netted her a lucrative contract as the 'face' of Estée Lauder cosmetics, followed by a string of film roles although some of them were admittedly dreadful. 1997, however, saw Liz Hurley starring in the movie *Austin Powers Man Of Mystery*, for which she had rave reviews . . .

It is piquant that Lili Maltese, the Hawaiian-born model and new girlfriend of Henry Dent Brocklehurst (the man who comforted Hurley in the wake of the Grant/Divine Brown affair and who has often been tipped as a successor to Grant in Hurley's affections), also wears Versace. Maltese, who bears a striking resemblance to Liz Hurley, says, 'Henry definitely approves of me wearing Versace.'

The pay-back for Versace was both overt – Annalisa Barbieri, Contributing Editor of the British *Independent on Sunday* newspaper says, 'As soon as he started using celebrities, well you could forget about any clever ad campaigns. He had the best advertising money could buy' – and more subtle. Stars such as Hurley not only flaunted his frocks at swishy events and lined his catwalk; they also added glamour to more private soirées. Sarah Walter remembers 'an intimate dinner for

300' in Paris after one of Versace's couture shows. 'Dinner was wonderful – risotto, some fish and fabulous desserts.' However, the food wasn't the point. 'There were all these *Hello!* people there.' Being able to guarantee a celebrity contingent for a party was a sure-fire way to generate press interest. Sly Stallone gyrating on a dance floor with Donatella was far too good a story to miss.' Versace had other methods of winning favour with the press, of course. 'After the Liz Hurley dress they [the Versace organization] began to court the British tabloid press. From being completely hideous, they became lovely which was much more scary,' says David Hayes, freelance stylist and former Fashion Editor of British *Today* newspaper. Catwalk photographer Christopher Moore remembers visiting the Versace showroom with one senior Fashion Editor. 'She was wearing a blazer and they said, "Oh, you must have one of ours" and took hers off her and gave her a Versace one,' Vicki Woods explains: 'In the first season you got ashtrays and scarves. Then, when they knew you, you moved up to suits.'

Woods was once the recipient of a spectacular Versace gift. The story begins at a dinner she gave in London, as Editor of British *Harpers & Queen* magazine, for the Versaces. 'We had rock stars for Donatella. She had Geldof on her table. Gianni was on mine,' Woods explains. Emmanuella Schmeidler, Versace's Head of International PR, arrived wearing one of Versace's gold mesh dresses. 'I said, "Oh, you look fabulous." Emmanuella was paranoid Gianni wouldn't enjoy himself. At the end of the evening she finally took a drink and said: "You like my gold dress? I send it to you,". .' Woods said she thought that they wouldn't have one in her size, to which Emman-uella replied: 'We make it for you.'

Woods subsequently left *Harpers & Queen* and forgot all about the dress. One day, many months later, she was at the hairdressers. 'A man came in with Versace bags the size of refrigerators. They weighed about the same as a refrigerator too,' she reveals. Woods waited until her hair was done and then opened the bags. 'I kept pulling out these pieces of indescribably heavy gold metal, plus a black barathea jacket to go over the top.' There was a note attached which read: 'With love from Gianni'. When Woods got home she tried the dress on, 'And it f****** fitted,' she says. 'I rang the PR and said "How much did this cost?". She said, "Oh, for couture, about $35,000, darling".

So was this bribery? 'It wasn't *payola*. it was because they were nice,' says Woods. 'It's the Italian way. You invite someone English to dinner and they will send you a note afterwards. An Italian will bring a gift, beautifully wrapped.' What made Woods' gift all the more remarkable was that she was no longer in a position to do Versace any good. Yet, they still gave her the dress. Why? 'Because they were like that. If you were a friend you were a friend,' explains Woods.

Before her own tragic death just six weeks after her friend, probably the woman who had become Versace's most famous

*The king of frock
'n' roll.
(Top left) Gianni
with Liz Tilberis,
editor of U.S.
Harpers Bazaar
and Karl
Lagerfeld
(Bottom left) With
George Michael
and Elton John
(Above) Sting and
Trudie Styler's
wedding. Bride
and groom wore
Versace.*

Versace A-Z

Versace's home town of Reggio de Calabria has few links with the world of international fashion. But the plains to the north of the city are the only place in the world where Bergamot oranges are grown. Still squeezed by hand, the distilled essence is an essential ingredient in luxury perfumes, including those produced for Versace spA.

Orange
O is for Orange

(Left) That *dress, Liz Hurley and Hugh Grant 1994*
(Above) *Naomi in another version of* that *dress Spring/Summer 1994.*

client and confidante was the Princess of Wales. During her marriage to Prince Charles, Diana had been under considerable pressure to buy British with part of her royal role being to travel the world as a walking billboard for British fashion. However, the moment her marriage hit the rocks, she was able to indulge her real taste. She turned to Versace. However, while Gianni and Diana formed a warm friendship, it did suffer a severe hiccup over the publication of *Rock and Royalty*, Versace's glossy charity book.

The Princess agreed to write a foreword to the book. But when early copies were leaked to the press, there was an uproar. The book featured naked men and Diana panicked. She asked for her

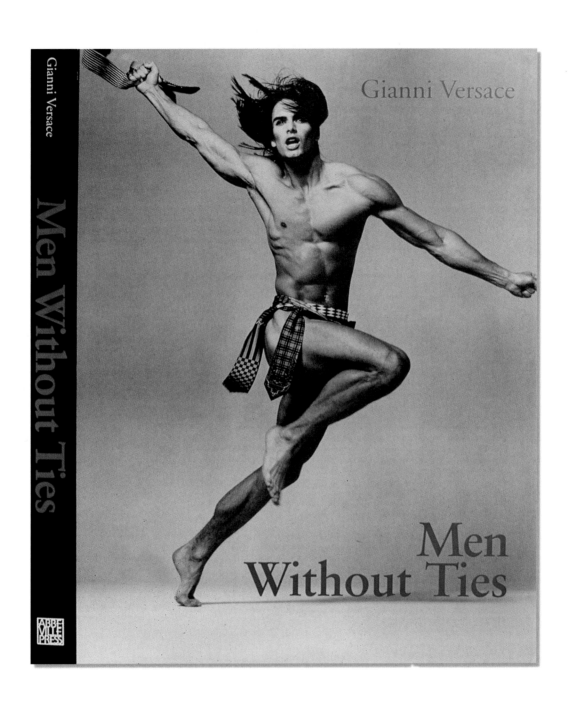

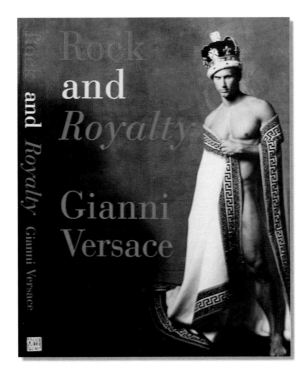

(Far left) **Man with ties, but not much else** *(Abbeville Press)*
(Left) **The look Prince Charles never modelled, from the front cover of** Rock and Royalty *(Abbeville Press)*
(Below) **The back cover of** Rock and Royalty *displays some of Gianni's inspiration.*

foreword to be removed. Versace had the entire print run pulped, at a cost of many thousands of dollars. The published version contains only a short quote from the Princess: 'Gianni Versace is an aesthete, in search of the essence of beauty, which he captures with grace and ease. From the optimism that shines from the pages of this book one can tell he loves mankind.'

In the fashion world, Versace was unusual, if not unique, in demonstrating genuine loyalty to those he had come to think of as friends. A clever businessman, he knew the value of keeping celebrities and magazine editors sweet, but he was also Calabrian to the core. Once someone had penetrated the psychological walls with which he, Donatella and Santo surrounded themselves, he was intensely loyal. Elton John, Madonna, Sly and Jennifer, Sting and Trudie — these people were not just walking, talking advertising hoardings for the Versace brand, they also became a sort of extended family for Versace.

He didn't just meet them for fittings; he also welcomed them into his homes. And what homes they were . . . GV

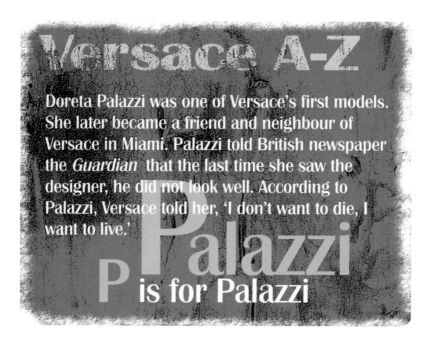

Versace A-Z

Doreta Palazzi was one of Versace's first models. She later became a friend and neighbour of Versace in Miami. Palazzi told British newspaper the *Guardian* that the last time she saw the designer, he did not look well. According to Palazzi, Versace told her, 'I don't want to die, I want to live.'

Palazzi

P is for Palazzi

*Rock goddess
in Versace;
Madonna at
the 1995 Brit
Awards.*

Interiors

An emperor needs a palace. Gianni Versace had four. As befits the man who dressed Supermodels in liquid gold chain mail and pop stars in psychedelic diamanté, they were all stupendously lavish. If there was a marble floor, it would be the best Italian marble; if there was a painting, it would be a Picasso. The contrast between ancient and modern as seen on Versace's catwalk was expressed in his homes in a fantastical mix of Corinthian columns and broken crockery canvasses by Julian Schnabel. If one home had a Jane Austen-style formal English garden, then another boasted a *Dynasty*-style swimming pool . . .

Each of Versace's palaces marked a different point in his life and career. The first was the Villa Fontanelle on the shore of Lake Como. Far enough away from Milan to represent a genuine retreat, it was nevertheless a long way from spartan. In *Do Not Disturb*, the book devoted somewhat ironically to throwing open the doors of his private, inner sanctums, Versace wrote of his homes: 'Inside you can create your own perfect dimensions of taste, beauty and harmony to reflect your image and personality.' It was at the Villa Fontanelle that Gianni began to create the world he had always dreamed of living in. All those

Donatella and daughter Allegra.

'I slept in Gianni Versace's bed. Of course he wasn't in it at the time.'

Madonna

boyhood trips to the Museo Nazionale della Magna Gecia in Reggio de Calabria have borne fruit at Villa Fontanelle. It is a palace of which the most opulent Roman emperor would be truly proud.

Villa Fontanelle was originally built for English Lord Currie in the nineteenth century, which accounts for the English-style garden. Unable to find a house he liked in the area, Lord Currie bought an abandoned quarry of local Moltrasio stone which he used to build first a smaller house, The Palazzetto (little palace), before constructing the Villa Fontanelle. The house passed through various hands, including those of the Cambiaghi Counts, before the Versace family bought and restored it in 1980.

The Villa Fontanelle is everything that an Italian Palazzo is supposed to be — and then some. It is grand, gracious and, above all, fabulously luxurious. Villa Fontanelle has large rooms with high ceilings, sweeping staircases, gorgeous frescos, gleaming inlaid marble floors and enough chandeliers to outshine Las Vegas. That is not to say it is in poor

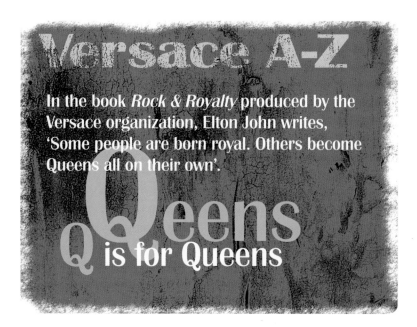

In the book *Rock & Royalty* produced by the Versace organization, Elton John writes, 'Some people are born royal. Others become Queens all on their own'.

Queens
Q is for Queens

taste — quite the opposite. The antique furniture with which Gianni filled it is impeccable and of a profusion well beyond the financial reach of even the most wealthy aristocrat. Brocade-covered sofas sit next to Napoleonic side tables, groaning with neoclassical knick-knacks. Walls are hung with old masters and depictions of ancient Greece. There are some modern touches, too. Vibrant rugs have been hand-woven in Versace's trademark baroque style and finished with a Greco-Roman border and the stair carpet is in a similar vein.

Still, if the house is a celebration of Versace's taste, he was generous with his hospitality. Fashion historian Colin McDowell wrote of Versace in the London

Sunday Times: 'He presided over a large and glamorous coterie with which few could compete.' And there was something of the Medici in Gianni Versace. He was a fashion designer but his interests were much wider. At Villa Fontanelle, and later at his other homes, he liked to gather a diverse collection of people, from pop stars to ballet dancers, for spectacular dinner parties. His parallel career as a costume designer meant that he had many friends in the theatre, but he might just as easily invite a sports star as an opera diva. On one occasion, he seated Liz Tilberis, Editor of American *Harpers Bazaar* magazine, next to an Italian footballer for dinner. What on earth did they chat about between courses — the latest cut of soccer shorts?

Versace was also happy to lend Villa Fontanelle to his friends. Madonna was among many of his showbiz pals who stayed there. She wrote in *Time* magazine: 'I slept in Gianni Versace's bed. Of course, he wasn't in it at the time, but I couldn't help feeling that I was soaking up some of his aura.' Versace's bedroom at the Lake Como House was filled with books, paintings and statues of Greek gods. And according to Madonna: 'They could have been important Greek gods or just your standard Roman hunks, but they were lovely to look at and very distracting.'

During Madonna's stay, she was treated 'like a Princess'. Every morning, Italian bodyguards took her pet dog, Chiquita, for a walk, in between delivering fresh batches of Versace dresses to her. Then, every evening at sunset, Madonna and friends were served fresh Bellinis by Sri Lankan waiters in white gloves, under a giant magnolia tree at the edge of the lake. A speedboat was on perma- nent standby in case any of the party fancied a swim. 'We had to pinch ourselves to make sure we weren't dreaming.' she wrote. 'I

was envious of a person who had the courage to live life so luxuriously.' Coming from *The Material Girl*, whose own place in Miami is hardly a hovel, that's saying something.

Next to be added to the Versace property portfolio was the Palazzo Rizzoli on Via Gesu, in the heart of Milan's designer fashion district. Milan is an overwhelmingly modern city. Its architecture is dull and even oppressive. However, the windy Via Gesu is part of the old city, an historic haven in the midst of square-built apartment blocks. The street gets its name from the convent built for Franciscan nuns that once occupied a corner site. Palazzo Rizzoli sits at number twelve. Rizzoli is a reference to the family who bought it after World War Two and established a gallery of contemporary art there on the ground floor.

By the time Versace had purchased the Palazzo Rizzoli his business was doing well. He needed both a home and a swanky HQ in Milan. The Versace family bought the first chunk of the three storey, nineteenth- century Palazzo Rizzoli in 1982, and the rest in 1986. Gianni kept a private apartment on the

The fantastic opulence of Casa
Casuarina, Florida;
(Left) Donatella's bathroom
(Below) Her bedroom.

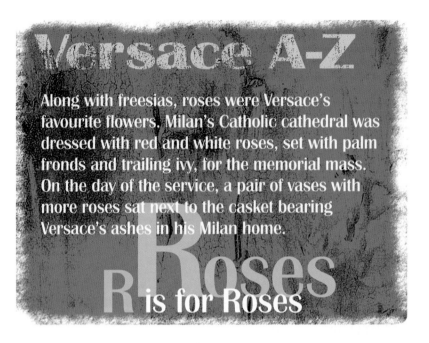

Along with freesias, roses were Versace's favourite flowers. Milan's Catholic cathedral was dressed with red and white roses, set with palm fronds and trailing ivy, for the memorial mass. On the day of the service, a pair of vases with more roses sat next to the casket bearing Versace's ashes in his Milan home.

R is for Roses

second floor of the left wing. The remainder of the building is occupied by offices and his haute couture 'Atelier' workrooms.

The interior is on a less monumental scale than the Villa Fontanelle and it has a cosier air. Polished oak panelling, ornate plasterwork walls and furniture covered in Gianni's own voluptuous prints give it a warmth. Palazzo Rizzoli's most outstanding feature is a secret garden on the roof. Small and triangular, it overlooks a courtyard two floors below. A balustrade is lined with terracotta pots filled with clipped box and one wall is covered in antique fountain heads. Gianni enjoyed giving dinner parties up there. Guests were led through the library of his private

apartment and out through doors to an arbour. On either side of the doors are lemon trees. As the party ate and drank, the scent of citrus was mixed with that of climbing jasmine.

With Palazzo Rizzoli and Villa Fontanelle, Versace had constructed two of the most extraordinary private palaces in the world. Still, something was missing. For, if there was a side to Versace that craved quiet and serenity, there was another that, to paraphrase Cindi Lauper, just wanted to have fun. By the turn of the 1990s, he was at the height of his career. He had worked hard and achieved wealth and fame and now it was time to cut loose.

Donatella was the first to discover Miami. In 1991 she was

(Above) *The maestro at work*
(Left) *Relaxing at Sylvester Stallone's house-warming party.*

One of the earliest pop stars to be dressed by Versace, Bruce Springsteen became a close friend. When, in 1985, Springsteen married Julianne Phillips, Versace provided a suitably romantic setting for the honeymoon. He loaned them the Villa Fontanelle on Lake Como. Sadly, Mr and Mrs Springsteen are no longer together.

Springsteen
is for Springsteen

on holiday there with her husband Paul Beck and their two children, Allegra and Daniel. (These are two of the most photogenic children on earth and she could not have found a better gene pool than that provided by Beck, former model and close friend of Gianni, who is now in charge of directing Versace's advertising campaigns.) As the family relaxed in the sun, Donatella tried to persuade Gianni to join them. Finally, Gianni and his long-time partner Antonio D'Amico decided to stop off on their way to Cuba.

When Versace arrived, he was intrigued by the area. He hired a driver to show him around and ended up on South Beach. He told *Time* magazine: 'I said to my friend [D'Amico], "Why do we

have to go to Cuba? It's fun here." It was love at first sight.' It's not difficult to see what Gianni found so alluring about South beach. Anyone taking a stroll is liable to get mown down by boys on rollerblades in hotpants. Author Michaelangelo Signole told *Time* magazine: 'For Versace, South Beach was all about his belief in the body beautiful — all those beautiful young men who originally influenced his fashion, partying outside his front door.'

Some have pointed to the sleazy side of South Beach and questioned why a designer of Versace's international reputation should have wanted to live within ten miles of the place. But, as with London's Soho and New York's Greenwich Village, a touch of sleaze can be what gives an area character. South Beach businessman Eugene Parton told the British *Mail on Sunday* newspaper: 'He loved the opportunities that South Beach gave him for being public. It was part of the allure of living there.' The manager of the local night-club, The Warsaw Ballroom, also commented: 'He didn't want to live on an island, isolated like other designers'

Versace bought a run-down apartment building, the Amsterdam Palace, in 1992. Although the address is 1116 on Miami's Art Deco Ocean Drive, its look is less sleek 1930s than old Hollywood Spanish. It was built for Charles D. Boulton, a success-ful landscape architect and a man with a taste for flamboyant gestures. The original name, to which Versace reverted, was Casa Casuarina which Boulton borrowed from a book of short stories by Somerset Maugham, *The Casuarina Tree*, because a lone Australian Casuarina tree sat on the site during construction, reminding him of the tale.

The model for the house was a castle built in Santo Domingo by Christopher Columbus's son, Diego Columbus. A brick from that castle is buried in the foundations of Casa Casuarina and a coat of arms from the Columbus family tomb also decorates the front terrace. One last and slightly macabre touch is the tower to one side of the patio, which is a replica of the prison in which Christopher Columbus was held. Still, if Charles D. Boulton was a man of considerable architectural flair, Giannni Versace more than matched him during his renovations to the house.

Estimates as to how much Gianni spent on Casa Casuarina vary. Some put the bill as high as $40 million and the finished effect is remarkable — Spanish kitsch with gold classical knobs on. The interior features mosaiced walls, Greco—Roman friezes, inlaid floors, frescoed ceilings and stunning stained glass windows. All around are Versace's rich fabrics, mixed with more gold and leopard print. Outside, the house is arranged around a small garden, dominated by a swimming pool whose floor is tiled in imitation of

A Roman bath fit for an Emperor, the swimming pool at Casa Casuarina.

Casa Casuarina; (Top) *The Emperor's inner sanctum, Gianni's bedroom*
(Bottom) *Entertaining in style, the dining room.*

Versace A-Z

Miami sandwich shop worker, G. Kenneth Brown, told *Time* magazine that four days before Versace's murder Andrew Cunanan came into his shop for a tuna sub sandwich. Recognizing him, Brown went into the kitchen and dialled 911. Unfortunately, another member of staff took Cunanan's $4.12, and, before police could reach the shop, Cunanan disappeared. When Brown learned of the designer's murder, he said, 'I wanted to throw up. I was thinking, if only they had caught him, Versace might still be alive.'

Tuna
is for Tuna

one of Gianni's famous scarf prints. It's a coin's toss which is the more outrageous: the Villa Fontanelle or Casa Casuarina. Both are so stuffed with bijoux details that they almost make your head spin.

For Gianni Versace, Casa Casuarina was the ultimate holiday home. From the roof, Versace had a good view of South Beach (plus that of the rather less attractive rubbish-strewn vacant lot next door).

Modelling wannabes were in the habit of hanging about outside the mansion. Very occasionally, Versace would pluck a lucky face from out of the crowd to appear in one of his advertising campaigns.

Versace's arrival in South Beach did much to lift the area. Indeed, many of the local café owners have much to thank their famous neighbour for. Gianni was a highly visible resident, often entertaining on a grand scale. Numerous charity bashes were held at Casa Casuarina and, for the last two years he threw a New Year's Eve party there. He was also a regular visitor to Miami's gay nightclubs, with his arrival invariably being announced over the PA system.

Still, to class Versace as a hedonist is to misrepresent him.

The member of the Versace family who really enjoys partying is Donatella. As was once said of her: 'She dances with Kate Moss at hip New York nightclubs and goes laden with gifts for Madonna's baby.' It is Donatella who does most of the socializing with Sting, Cher, Lisa-Marie Presley and George Michael.

To an extent, her interest is professional. As Gianni explained to *Kaleidoscope* magazine, Donatella 'takes her cues from the musical world, from rock stars and the stars who have become her friends.' When Gianni entertained, dinner parties ended promptly at 11pm, and according to designer Janei Smith, he much preferred being at home. She told *Time* magazine that he once said to her: 'You can go to a restaurant if you want, but things are always better at home.' But which one? Gianni had yet to add another palace to his empire . . .

Versace had already added a

A very private partnership; Gianni and longtime companion Antonio D'Amico, in Florence, June 1997.

secret pied-à-terre in London in 1992. It was on the top floor of his Old Bond Street flagship store and, although tiny, it boasted all the Versace interior design trimmings. 'It was as if Bond Street was too tasteful for him. He needed a retreat from it,' says Heath Brown, Fashion Editor of the London *Times* newspaper. What Versace now needed was a base in New York. Florida may have been fun, but to do business in the USA, the Big Apple was where he had to be. Gianni found a house on the fashionable Upper East Side and set about transforming it in his own inimitable style.

Walking into the house, you enter a large hall with stairs and an elevator on your left. The elevator might sound a bit excessive, but the house is tall and narrow. Five floors is a lot to climb if you don't have to. The main reception room is lavishly appointed with a couple of Corinthian columns and paintings covering every wall. It leads to a huge garden. Upstairs are the bedrooms, with the dining room on the top floor. Every room bears the signature of a different artist, from Francesco Clemente to Julian Schnabel.

Journalist and author Henry Porter visited the house. 'I particularly remember a Picasso in Versace's bedroom, a portrait of a woman from the late Cubist period. It was astonishingly beautiful. All grey and green and white, and about two feet square. It really was a very desirable painting,' he says. Porter was also struck by the other Picassos downstairs, the Miro and a Fernand Léger. 'The Léger was particularly stunning,' he remembers. 'There were so many paintings — and these things cost 15 to 20 million dollars each.'

Porter ended up in Versace's bedroom after going off in search of a bathroom. 'The only one I could find was concealed in some panelling in the bedroom,' he explains. 'It was a tiny closet room, with a loo and a sink, but no bath. There was a fiddly little catch on the inside. I got stuck and was hammering on the door for ages.' Porter managed to free himself and then had a good look round (well, you would, wouldn't you?). 'It really reminded me of one of those very dark rooms of Renaissance Italy. It had wonderful inlaid walls and lots of wood around. It was beautifully lit, very dim,' he says. 'There was no gold. It was superbly understated. It really was the best room in the house.'

It was at this point that Porter was disturbed by Gianni, plus bodyguard, who escorted him back up to dinner. Also there was Elton John in a black suit, Julian Schnabel, movie moguls Barry Diller and David Geffen, Calvin and Kelly Klein, Graydon Carter, Editor of *Vanity Fair* and Anna Wintour, Editor of American *Vogue*. 'This was a business dinner in the sense of wowing people who needed to be wowed,' explains Porter. The food was simple, peasant Italian.

After dinner, Elton John gave a concert at a grand piano that had been specially brought in and Jon Bon Jovi arrived. Hugh Grant and Liz Hurley also dropped in.

Hurley was smoking and Porter saw her tip her ash on the floor. 'I don't think she knew she was doing it, but because I'm a smoker and I hadn't had a cigarette because I couldn't see where to put my ash, I noticed and I'm sure Versace noticed too,' Porter says. Did Gianni not berate Hurley for treading ash into his beautiful floor? 'I think he had a quiet word and someone brought an ashtray,' Porter explains. Apparently Gianni was a genial host. 'A very nice man,' is how Porter puts it.

Still, if he enjoyed these sorts of soirées, he was at heart reserved, even shy. In his book *Do Not Disturb*, Versace described the satisfaction all his homes gave him. He chose the title because: 'It is the phrase which best describes my feelings of home, a refuge to which I retreat in search of serenity, tranquillity and comfort. Reality stays outside.'

But reality wasn't going to stay outside: it was just about to make a brutal intrusion upon the gilded life of Gianni Versace and his family . . . ⓖⓥ

The Legend Lives On

At 8.30 on the morning of Tuesday 15 July 1997 Gianni Versace was returning home. He hadn't been far, just the usual few blocks to the nearby NewsCafé on Ocean Drive for a coffee and a look to see if they had any new magazines. His partner, Antonio D'Amico, was waiting for him inside Casa Casuarina. Just a few moments more and Versace too would have been safely inside. Instead of this, as he pushed open the intricate wrought iron gates to his Miami mansion, he was gunned down.

Witnesses disagree about what happened. A white man in his twenties was seen with Versace outside Casa Casuarina. Some onlookers describe a struggle over a bag. Others say Versace and the man exchanged a few words. Miami resident, Romeo Jacques, told *Time*, magazine: 'The next thing I know, I heard pow pow, and I ducked to the ground.' The man had shot Versace once in the back of the head and again as he lay on the ground. He then ran off down Ocean Drive, pursued by one brave witness. The attacker turned, pointed the gun at his pursuer, didn't fire it, and then disappeared quickly.

Without doubt Gianni Versace was seriously hurt. As he lay bleeding on the steps of his Florida home, D'Amico ran out and did his best to revive him. But it was too late. Versace was rushed to Miami's Jackson Memorial Hospital where he was declared dead. Back at Casa Casuarina, police were throwing a cordon round the murder scene, being careful not to disturb the pool of blood now marring the once-pristine front steps. Next to this gory reminder of what had happened sat Gianni Versace's designer sandals, adding a surreal poignancy to the scene. Within twenty-four hours, the FBI announced that they had a prime suspect. He was Andrew Phillip Cunanan, twenty-seven year-old college drop-out and one-time gigolo from San Diego.

Examination of the bullets that had killed Versace revealed that they had come from the same gun, a Golden Sabre .4 calibre pistol. The FBI believed Cunanan had it used to murder two other men: David Madson in Minnesota and William Reese, a cemetery caretaker from New Jersey. Cunanan was also wanted in connection with two other killings, those of Jeffrey Trail and Lee Miglin. Trail's body was found

in Madson's apartment, beaten to death with a claw hammer, while Lee Miglin, a Chicago business-man, had been discovered wrapped in duct tape, with a space left so that he could breathe, under a car in the garage of his Gold Coast home. He had been stabbed with garden shears and his throat cut with a garden saw. The killer had a snack of an apple and some ham before stealing Miglin's green 1994 Lexus car.

Cunanan was clearly a very dangerous man. He was also an exceedingly stupid one. Either that, or he wanted to get caught. When Trail's body was found at

A beaded goodbye from Versace *Spring/Summer 1990.*

(Left) *Boys, boys, boys ... Versace menswear* Spring/Summer 1997
(Below) *Relaxing at the Villa Fontanelle, from* **Do Not Disturb** (Abbeville Press)
(Right) *Simply stunning: Helena in white* Autumn/Winter 1995.

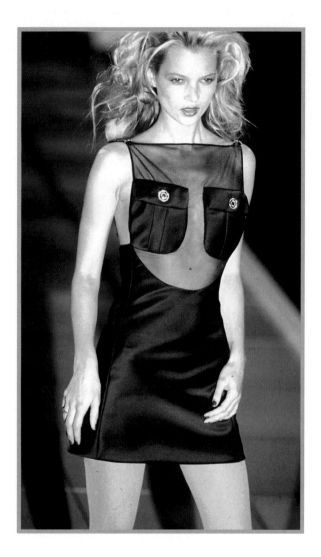

(Left) **Kate after her Versace makeover**
Autumn/Winter 1996
(Above) **Stella in red leather**
Autumn/Winter 1995.

Madson's apartment, police also discovered a gym bag with Cunanan's name on it and half a box of Golden Sabre .4 bullets. There was a message on Trail's answerphone from Cunanan asking him to come to Madson's apartment. After Versace's death, Reese's red 1995 Chevrolet pick-up (for which he had swapped the Lexus) was found in a Miami car park. The plates had been changed for ones stolen in a K-mart car park in Florence, southern California. Inside the car were Cunanan's passport, a cheque with his name on it, a pair of glasses, a jacket and wallet

Versace A-Z

The Versace empire was built upon riotously luxurious clothing. However, in his book *Men Without Ties*, Gianni wrote, 'A tuxedo alone cannot make you elegant, while even a pair of underpants can be worn with style.'

Underpants
U is for Underpants

Gianni's Miami hideaway, Casa Casuarina minutes after the brutal slaying.

Versace A-Z

Gianni Versace once recounted the tale of a visit that he and Donatella made to the all-pink home of legendary *Vogue* Editor Diana Vreeland. On meeting Donatella (who was then only twenty), Vreeland exclaimed, 'We have the same initials, perhaps some day you too will work in fashion.' Donatella subsequently sent Ms Vreeland some leather jeans and shirts that Gianni had designed. Vreeland mailed back snaps of herself wearing them. Gianni commented, 'One must never believe that an older woman cannot wear certain things.'

V is for Vreeland

belonging to Miglin, and a ticket stub from a pawn shop where Cunanan had pawned one of Miglin's gold coins. According to some especially lurid press reports, Cunanan had written Versace's name in blood inside the car.

Still, if Cunanan wasn't very bright, the police didn't appear to have been over-burdened with intelligence either. Cunanan had been featured on 'America's Most Wanted' five times. He had been floating around Miami for two months before the day of Versace's death. When police later searched room 205 at the $39-a-night Normandy Plaza hotel, they found a pair of electric clippers and some fashion magazines. The red Chevrolet he had stolen from Reese had been in the Miami car park for five weeks. The night before he is said to have murdered Versace, Cunanan ate ostrich, smoked trout and filet mignon at the fashionable California Cuisine restaurant in Miami. Still, he hadn't been caught. The FBI described him as a master of disguise and even suggested that he might have escaped capture after murdering Versace by dressing as a woman. 'He may have shaved off all his body hair to enhance this appearance,' explained an FBI spokesman. None of this, of course, explained why Cunanan may have done it. Wild theories circulated. Cunanan, it was suggested, was a disaffected ex-boyfriend of Versace. A former friend of Cunanan, Los Angeles attorney Eric Gruenwald, told *Time* magazine he was at a San Francisco nightclub with Cunanan when the latter announced: 'I just met Gianni Versace'. Gruenwald says he replied, 'Sure, and I'm Coco Chanel'. Other sources report that Versace and Cunanan might have met either at Lake Como or backstage at the San Francisco opera. Another theory put forward by the FBI was that Cunanan had AIDS and was just out to get even with the world. A hit list of other celebrities, including Madonna and Julio Iglesias, was another item said to have been found in his car. What is certain is that Andrew Cunanan was an unstable personality. The youngest of the four children raised by Modesto Cunanan, a Filipino sugar planter turned banker and his wife Mary-Ann, Cunanan was born on 31 August 1969. He was raised in a well-to-do suburb of San Diego. At the Bishop's School in La Jolla, he is remembered as popular, if attention seeking. As a teenager,

he was openly gay. He majored in history at the University of California before dropping out after his father returned to the Philippines to evade arrest on suspicion of the misappropriation of $106,000 from his stock brokerage firm. When asked about his son after Versace's murder, Modesto Cunanan said, 'My son is not like that. He had a Catholic upbringing. He was an altar boy'.

Altar boy or not, Andrew Cunanan was a compulsive liar. Living off a variety of rich men who furnished him with fancy cars and even fancier clothes, although not those designed by Versace – Cunanan's style was more baseball cap and sweatshirt preppy. He told anyone he met that he owned a factory either in Mexico or the Philippines, depending upon his mood. Cunanan also adopted the name Andrew DeSilva and fabricated a wife and daughter, going as far as to hand round a supposed snapshot of his fictitious family. San Diego barman Tim Barthell told the British *Mirror* newspaper: 'He was a very loud guy. No-one ever punched him or anything,

(Above) *Sheer Glamour. Kate on the catwalk*
Spring/Summer 1996
(Right, top) *Naomi looking regal*
Autumn/Winter 1997
(Right, bottom) *Kate almost dressed*
Autumn/Winter 1997.

although I know some guys who thought about it'. When his last boyfriend dumped him, Cunanan began drinking heavily, adding vodka to his customary cranberry juice. He was $46,000 in debt, his looks were on the slide and there was no sign of a sugar daddy to bail him out.

Still, none of this proves that Cunanan killed Versace. The FBI may think they got their man but even after Cunanan was found dead, shot through the head, on a Miami houseboat on 23 July after a four-hour police siege, questions remain. If it was suicide, why was there no suicide note? If Cunanan used the same Golden Sabre .4 calibre pistol to shoot himself as he had to kill Versace (as the FBI insist), why was it that Versace's wounds were so much cleaner than his own? Cunanan was so badly disfigured that he could not immediately be identified by police. And what about the mysterious second figure that was seen moving about on the boat as police surrounded it, or the second shot some witnesses claim to have heard as police stormed it?

At least one man is not buying the lone AIDS serial killer story. Frank Monte, a New York private detective, claims Gianni Versace hired him to look into the murder of a friend. He believes both Versace and Cunanan were murdered by the Mafia. According to Monte, Cunanan's presence in Miami was a convenient smoke-screen for a Mob hit. He even suggests that Cunanan was killed before Versace and the former's body stored in a freezer until the time was right for it to be found. Monte told the British *Sunday Telegraph* newspaper: 'It is very convenient for the FBI to say otherwise because they get to clean up five murders'.

We may never know the truth. But, while all these rumours and counter-rumours were circulating, the Versace family had to deal with the certainty of Gianni's death. A funeral had to be arranged and this was tricky. On the one hand, the Versaces wanted to grieve privately. Always a tight-knit family, in such a crisis their instincts were Calabrian. They wanted to draw together as a family and repel outsiders. On the other hand, however, tributes from Gianni's former fashion and showbiz friends were pouring in.

Sly Stallone declared himself 'heartbroken', as did Boy George. Liz Hurley said, 'Gianni was a very

dear friend. He was massively talented and it is an appalling thing to have happened'. Claudia Schiffer told French *Elle* magazine: 'He was not only a gifted and talented couturier with whom it was extraordinary to work, he was also a marvelous, attentive man'. According to Naomi Campbell, 'His gift for friendship was as deep as his loyalty. In eleven years, he didn't do a single collection without me. He'd truly made me a member of his family'. These people wanted to be able to pay their last respects. As Gianni's life had been stolen from him in such a brutal way, there was also a desire to mark his achievements in a public way.

In the end, the Versace family decided on a compromise: a private funeral and a public memorial mass. Keeping the funeral private was going to be a feat, of course. Press interest was enormous. Santo and Donatella had Gianni's body cremated in Miami and then quietly boarded a Challenger 800 aircraft and flew to a small airport in northern Italy where they swapped to a helicopter for the next leg of the journey to Lake Como. The police and a battery of private security guards had sealed off Villa Fontanelle and the nearby cemetery. Santo and Donatella roared through the gates of the Villa in a Mercedes. The rest of the family gathered inside.

It had been Gianni's wish that he should be buried in the grounds of his beloved Villa Fontanelle. However, while in the past such an arrangement was customary within wealthy Italian families, now no amount of money or influence could facilitate such a thing. Donatella and Santo applied to the Mayor of Moltrasio for permission and were turned down. Mayor Celestino Villa was apologetic, but his hands were tied. Italian law prohibited it. 'One thing is certain: The urn will remain here with us on the shores of Lake Como. That was his wish,' Celestino announced. First, though, it had to be transported to Milan.

The memorial service for a man who lived such a gilded and

Versace A-Z

Anna 'Nuclear' Wintour, sunglassed Editor of American *Vogue*, is said to have suffered a fashion crisis on her way to attend Versace's memorial service in Milan. Her luggage failed to arrive at Linate airport. Only a hurried phone call to the Versace boutique averted disaster. A suitably sombre outfit was dispatched to Ms Wintour's hotel.

W is for Wintour

glamorous life was always liable to turn into a circus. Even without the sensational manner of his death, here was an occasion when an enormous number of the famous and the famously beautiful were to be concentrated in one place. TV, newspapers and magazines geared themselves up to capture celebrity tears en masse. Plus this was, above all, a memorial to a fashion emperor. White may have been Gianni's favourite colour – after his murder all the window displays of the Versace boutiques were changed to feature simple white gowns – but the fashion pack love an excuse to wear black. The opportunity to get oneself up in something flatteringly funereal, drape a veil dramatically over one's head and clutch a crucifix

was bound to prove too tantalizing for some.

The memorial service was arranged for 6pm on 22 July 1997 at Milan's Catholic cathedral, the Duomo. In the days beforehand, speculation as to who would attend reached hysteria level. Madonna, it was said, had booked herself a suite at The Four Seasons, next door to American *Vogue* Editor, Anna Wintour. George Michael was coming and Tina Turner was to jam with Sting and Elton, it was rumoured. In the end, Madonna, Michael and Turner didn't attended the mass. But so many others did. Private planes from across the world descended on Milan's Linate airport.

It is a tragic irony that the most high profile mourner was

the Princess of Wales. Just six weeks before the world grieved her own death, she famously comforted Elton John at Versace's memorial mass.

That this and other images were captured by at least one photographer, allowed into the church during the mass may seem peculiar. Perhaps the Versace family felt that one would get in anyway and they might as well have some control over who it was. Then again, maybe this was entirely in keeping with the life of the man whose every move was accompanied by a flashbulb.

Diana was among the first to arrive at the Palazzo Rizzoli, wearing a simple black Versace dress and jacket. She was greeted by Donatella and Norena, Gianni's sixty-five-year old cousin and honorary mother, at the house. A room had been set aside for Gianni's ashes. They were in a gold box, set on lace cloth on a table with a silver-framed photo of the designer, a copy of his book *Do Not Disturb* and a gold crucifix. A simple vase of white roses sat on either side of Versace's ashes. The room was kept dim, the yellow curtains pulled tightly closed and the only light provided by two candelabra

fitted with twelve candles. The Princess spent several minutes in the room before adjourning to another to change into a new black Versace dress with a short skirt, slit at the front and a simple string of pearls.

Elton John, in black Versace suit, black tee-shirt and diamond-shaped glasses, spent thirty minutes (some of it weeping),

A sombre Kristen McMenemy on the Versace runway Spring/Summer 1997.

Very Versace. Claudia in spangles Spring/Summer 1995.

paying his respects to Gianni at the house. Naomi Campbell flew in from Johannesburg and arrived by chauffeur-driven Mercedes. When it became trapped in the mêlée of police and mourners outside, Naomi waved frantically at her driver to get her through the throng. On the walk from the

Herzigova and new face Esther Canadis, in black tee-shirt and flares, arrived. One hundred workers from the Versace factory outside Milan had also travelled by bus to honour their former boss, although they went straight to the Duomo. Versace boutiques across the world were closed for

"He was not only a gifted and talented couturier, he was also a marvellous, attentive man."

Claudia Schiffer

car to the house, Naomi (in another veil), staggered and almost fell. She had to be supported by Versace's minder Bruno – who, like all the security men, wore a black Versace suit and dark glasses – offered words of encouragement. 'Let's go, you can do it,' he said. She was lead upstairs by Santo.

Sting and Trudie (yet another veil), Italian ski star Alberto Tomba and a set of Supermodels, including Carla Bruni, Eva

the day and, as a further mark of respect, the Via della Spiga, the street on which Gianni launched his fashion career, was closed for an hour during the service.

Alexandra Shulman attended the mass. 'It was very emotional, very moving. Very Italian, very black and serious,' she says. 'It was much quieter than it looked'. How it looked was like nothing so much as one of Gianni Versace's fashion shows, albeit one showing an uncharacteristically funereal

Versace A-Z

Before Michael Hutchence so cruelly dumped Helena Christensen for the more mature charms of Mrs Bob Geldof (aka Paula Yates), the InXs frontman was a regular fixture at Versace fashion shows. So devoted was he to his Supermodel girlfriend that he would be happy to loiter backstage for hours beforehand. Versace returned the favour by giving him a front row seat and playing his current hit during the show, the latter making Michael squirm ever so slightly.

X is for InXs

collection. Crash barriers were erected round the fourteenth century church and a three-tier entry system put into operation. Four hundred close friends received hastily-printed invitations in handwritten envelopes with numbers on the back. Those without these all-important pieces of card were kept behind the crash barriers. People with 'ordinary' tickets went in through the front door while celebrities, including Carolyn Bessette, wife of John F. Kennedy Junior, were provided with a separate side entrance.

Inside the church, the parallel with a fashion show was just as marked. Seating was arranged according to status and personal relationship with the dead designer. The Princess of Wales sat between Elton John and Trudie Styler in the family pew with Antonio d'Amico, Santo, Donatella, Paul Beck and their children, Allegra and Daniel. To Elton's left was his lover David Furnish. Sting sat next to Trudie. Anna Wintour, for once, was bumped to the second row. Across the aisle was a roll call of fashion greats: Valentino, Gianfranco Ferre, Azzedine Alaia, Armani, the Missonis, Mariucca Mandelli of Krizia, Carla Fendi and Alberta Ferretta. Naomi sat with Eva Herzigova, Michelle Hicks, Carla Bruni and Esther Canadis. Sunglasses were produced when emotion became

Together forever.
Gianni and Donatella
on the catwalk
Autumn/Winter 1997.

Versace A-Z

Madonna was a neighbour of Versace's in Miami and a frequent visitor to his home. The last time she saw him, the pair discussed alternative therapies, Madonna recommending her yoga teacher. 'I could totally imagine this extravagant Calabrian with a twinkle in his eye in the Lotus position', she wrote in *Time* magazine.

Yoga
Y is for Yoga

too great. The most moving part of the service came when Sting and Elton John stood in front of a microphone set up beside the altar and sang the twenty-third Psalm, *The Lord is My Shepherd*. It had been doubtful as to whether Elton would manage it. He broke down when he entered the Duomo and wept openly.

The boy from southern Italy, who learned his craft in his mothers dress shop, got the closest thing to a State funeral Milan could manage. A princess had cried, pop stars had sung and outside the Duomo up to 10,000 mourners were gathered to pay their own respects. They didn't have tickets, but they came anyway. Some, certainly, had come to gawp. Others, though, were there because they genuinely felt something had died with Gianni on the steps of the Casa Casuarina. Except, of course, it didn't really die.

Gianni Versace bequeathed not simply a chorus line of gorgeous frocks to the world, he also created a new attitude. By blurring the line between fashion and showbiz, rock and royalty, art and commercialism, Gianni made haute couture fun and glamorous and accessible to millions. His attitude quite simply changed the face of fashion. As Madonna wrote in *Time*: 'Even though Gianni's life has ended, his spirit is everywhere and his soul lives forever'. **GV**

Mourning Gianni.
(Above, from left) *Sting, Trudie, Diana, Elton, David Furnish*
(Left) *And then there were two. Santo and Donatella outside the Duomo.*

1946-1997

Following an attempt to steal Gianni Versace's ashes, his tomb at Moltrasio is now protected by electronic alarms and guarded twenty-four hours a day. Even so, it has become a point of pilgrimage for fashion followers. 'Most are German and Japanese, but we also get French, English and, of course, Italian sightseers turning up', one local tour operator told Italy's *Corriere della Serra* newspaper. 'We are getting to the point where we are under pressure to include Versace's tomb as a highlight of our advertised tour programme'.

Picture Credits

Alpha – pages 41, 85 (bottom), 93
Alpha/Dave Benett – pages 42, 77, 85 (top left), 99 (bottom)
Alpha/Angeli – page 81 (left)
Alpha/M. Serota/Photolink – pages 97, 102, 103
Christopher Moore – pages 7, 11, 31, 32, 34 46, 47, 50, 52, 57, 59, 62,
63, 66, 67, 70, 71, 73, 74, 87, 109, 110, 111, 112, 116, 117, 120, 121, 123,
126, back cover
Rex Features – page 65, 86
Rex Features/Sipa Press – pages 19, 21, 27, 105, 125
Rex Features/Tim Rooke – page 81 (right)
Rex Features/Dave Hartley – page 85 (right)
Rex Features/Richard Young – front cover and page 91
Rex Features/Miami Herald – page 113
Rex Features/Steve Wood – page 125
Frank Spooner Pictures/Eric Brissaud – page 99 (top)

The author and publishers have made every reasonable effort to contact all copyright holders. Any
errors that may have occurred are inadvertent and anyone who for any reason has not been
contacted is invited to write to the publishers so that a full acknowledgement may be made in
subsequent editions of this work.

Versace A-Z

Diana, Princess of Wales, never looked more lovely than when she was wearing Versace. His genius was in making the most of her voluptuous curves, perhaps most famously when she sat next to Henry Kissinger at a dinner in New York and much comment was made on the appearance of her cleavage. This Gianni accomplished with an ingenious double-zip arrangement incorporated into Diana's evening gown. Inside many Atelier Versace dresses, there is a lining which is fitted tightly to the body. This lifts and holds — Wonderbra-style — allowing the dress proper to merely float on top.

Z is for Zip